THE REPUBLIC

The Odyssey of Philosophy

TWAYNE'S MASTERWORK STUDIES

Robert Lecker, General Editor

THE REPUBLIC

The Odyssey of Philosophy

Jacob Howland

TWAYNE PUBLISHERS NEW YORK
Maxwell Macmillan Canada • Toronto
Maxwell Macmillan International • New York Oxford Singapore Sydney

Twayne's Masterwork Studies No. 122

Twayne Publishers
Macmillan Publishing Company
866 Third Avenue
New York, New York 10022

Maxwell Macmillan Canada, Inc.
1200 Eglinton Avenue East
Suite 200
Don Mills, Ontario M3C 3N1

Library of Congress Cataloging-in-Publication Data
Howland, Jacob.
    The Republic : the odyssey of philosophy / Jacob Howland.
        p.   cm. — (Twayne's masterwork studies ; 122)
    Includes bibliographical references and index.
    ISBN 0-8057-8354-7 — ISBN 0-8057-8378-4 (pbk.)
    1. Plato. Republic. I. Title. II. Series.
JC71.P6H78 1993
321'.07—dc20
                                                                        93-17562
                                                                            CIP

The paper used in this publication meets the minimum requirements of American
National Standard for Information Sciences—Permanence of Paper for Printed Library
Materials, ANSI Z39.48-1984. ∞ ™

10 9 8 7 6 5 4 3 2 1 (alk. paper)
10 9 8 7 6 5 4 3 2 1 (pbk.: alk. paper)

Printed in the United States of America.

For Jennifer, Abraham, and Nathaniel

Contents

Note on the References
and Acknowledgments

Most *Republic* quotations are from *The Republic of Plato*, trans. Allan Bloom (New York: Basic Books, 1968); otherwise I offer my own translation. Except where noted, I have used the Greek text of James Adam, *The Republic of Plato*, 2 vols., 2d ed. (Cambridge: Cambridge University Press, 1963).

I am obliged to the Metropolitan Museum of Art, New York, for permission to reproduce on the dust jacket the *Panathenaic Prize Amphora: The Footrace* (Rogers Fund, 1914, 14.130.12) and for the frontispiece a black-and-white photograph of the *Panathenaic Prize Amphora: The Horserace* (Fletcher Fund, 1956, 56.171.3).

Part of Chapter 9 was adapted from my article "The Cave Image and the Problem of Place: The Sophist, the Poet, and the Philosopher," *Dionysius* 10 (1986): 21-55. I am grateful to the editors of *Dionysius* for permission to use this material.

I have dealt with terminology as follows. All Greek words are transliterated in the text. Unlike other familiar Greek words such as polis and logos, *erōs* appears in italics throughout in order to underscore its distinctive Platonic meaning. I have given convenient titles to Socrates' important myths and images, but it is occasionally useful to distinguish between a myth or image as a whole and a component that bears the same name. I have therefore capitalized Sun, Line, and Cave only when referring to the philosophical images of books 6 and 7 as distinct totalities; thus the cave wherein the prisoners reside is just one element—along with the fire, the shadows, and so on—of the image of the Cave. Similarly, the ring that renders its wearer invisible is the central component of the Myth of Gyges' Ring.

I would like to thank the following colleagues at the University of Tulsa for their support and encouragement during the preparation of this book: Paul Brown, Nicholas Capaldi, Austen Clark, Richard Lind, Richard McDonough, and Michael Patton. I am grateful to Charles Segal and Paul A. Rahe for much sound advice, and especially to my father-in-law, Henry V. Hayes, who read a rough version of the manuscript. Finally, I would like to thank the University of Tulsa for a Summer Faculty Development Fellowship in 1990, without which this study could not have been completed.

Panathenaic Prize Amphora: The Horserace (Fletcher Fund. 1956, 56.171.3)
Reproduced by permission of the Metropolitan Museum of Art, New York.

Chronology: Plato's Life and Works

All Dates are B.C.

ca. 750-700	The age of Homer and Hesiod. Rise of the polis—numerous small, independent, antimonarchic political communities—in Greece.
510-507	Fall of the Pisistratid tyranny in Athens; birth of the democratic Athenian republic.
480-479	Combined forces of the Greek cities defeat the invading army of the Persian empire at the battles of Salamis and Plataea, thereby saving the Greeks from foreign domination.
469	Socrates born in Athens to Sophroniscus, by legend a stonecutter, and Phaenarete.
461	Ascendancy of Pericles in Athens begins. During the Periclean age the Athenians extend their military and economic power, fortify the city, erect the Parthenon and other buildings, spend lavishly on sculptures and frescoes, and produce tragedies by Aeschylus, Sophocles, and Euripides.
431	A force of Thebans enters the town of Plataea, an ally of Athens. The Thebans are captured and put to death. This is the beginning of the Peloponnesian War between Athens and Sparta and their respective allies. The war will last for 27 years and bring about the downfall of the Athenian empire.
430	Farms of Athens burned by invading Peloponnesian armies. The Athenians, crowded together within the city walls, suffer from a deadly plague. Blaming Pericles for their misfortune, they suspend and fine him but later reinstate him.
429	Pericles dies in the plague.
ca. 428	Aristocles born on the island of Aegina to Ariston and Perictione, wealthy Athenians of noble ancestry. Aristocles is later called Plato from the Greek word for "broad," perhaps

	on account of the breadth of his forehead, his shoulders, or his literary style.
423	Aristophanes' *Clouds*, a comedy depicting Socrates as an irreligious natural philosopher and teacher of unjust rhetoric, is performed at the Festival Dionysia in Athens.
421-420	Approximate dramatic date of the *Republic*. The Athenian Nicias concludes a short-lived peace with Sparta. Alcibiades, the brilliant and ambitious orator and general portrayed in Plato's *Symposium, Alcibiades I* and *II*, and *Protagoras*, begins to dominate Athenian politics.
ca. 420	Plato begins to study grammar, music, poetry, mathematics, and wrestling with private teachers. He is extremely quick-witted and diligent, yet modest and sober in demeanor. He improves in wrestling and is a contender for the prize at the Isthmian Festival.
415	Alcibiades convinces the Athenians to launch a massive naval expedition to Sicily. Shortly before the expedition, the Athenians awaken to find that the statues of the protecting god Hermes, which were present throughout the city, have been mutilated. Alcibiades is implicated in the crime, as well as in the desecration of the Eleusinian Mysteries (secret rites of religious initiation), but is allowed to sail with the generals Lamachus and Nicias for Sicily. He is later recalled to Athens to stand trial, but he flees to Sparta, where he divulges valuable military secrets.
414-413	Lamachus dies. The Athenians are routed in battle by the Syracusans, but Nicias refuses to withdraw the troops because he interprets an eclipse of the moon as a bad omen. The navy is trapped in the harbor at Syracuse and annihilated.
413	Agis, the Spartan king, discovers that Alcibiades has slept with his wife. Alcibiades seeks refuge with the Persian satrap Tissaphernes and advises the Persians to play off Athens and Sparta against each other. Alcibiades nonetheless uses his influential position to aid Athens, so that he might gain favor in the eyes of his former countrymen.
411	The "Four Hundred," a group of oligarchs, take power in Athens. They are overthrown and democracy is restored after three months. The people call for the return of Alcibiades.
410	Plato, now 18, begins to serve a two-year tour of military duty as an ephebe, or adolescent citizen.

408	At this time Plato probably begins associating with Socrates and listening to his conversations in the public places of Athens. Plato is supposed to have written a number of poems and tragic plays but allegedly burns them after he glimpses the beauty of Socrates' soul. Alcibiades returns triumphantly to Athens and is elected general. He is feared by some citizens and is soon sent away from Athens into battle.
405-404	Athenians lose a crucial naval battle at Aegospotami. The Spartans blockade the Piraeus, Athens's harbor, and the Athenians are starved into submission. The Spartan conquerors install the "Thirty Tyrants," a ruthless oligarchical council led by Plato's relative Critias and including Charmides, Plato's uncle. Polemarchus and Niceratus, who appear in the *Republic*, are killed by the Thirty. Critias tells the Spartans that Alcibiades is a threat to the oligarchy. The Spartans hunt down Alcibiades and kill him in Phrygia.
404-403	A band of democrats seizes the Piraeus, and Critias and Charmides are killed in the ensuing battle. The Thirty Tyrants are deposed and democracy is eventually restored.
399	An Athenian court tries, convicts, and executes Socrates on the charges of not acknowledging the gods of Athens, introducing new and strange divinities, and corrupting the young. The restored democracy apparently holds Socrates partly responsible for the behavior of Alcibiades, Critias, and Charmides, all of whom frequented his company. After Socrates' execution, Plato leaves for Megara with other friends of Socrates. During the next 12 years he travels also to Cyrene in North Africa and to Egypt and Italy. He now begins to write and revise his dialogues, of which Socrates is the protagonist.
ca. 388	Plato makes the first of three visits to Sicily. He meets Dion, a relative of Dionysius I, the tyrant of Syracuse. Dion becomes a lifelong friend and supporter of Plato.
ca. 386	Plato begins to teach in a garden spot with shaded walks and a gymnasium near the sacred precinct of Academus. The school he founds here, the Academy, will continue in existence for 900 years. One of Plato's students is the philosopher Aristotle, who will later tutor Alexander the Great.
367	Dionysius I dies and is succeeded by his son, Dionysius II. Dion invites Plato to Syracuse in the hope that Dionysius II might be educated by Plato and become a "philosopher-king."

	Plato's visit fails and results in the exile of Dion. A later visit by Plato to Syracuse also fails to procure the restoration of Dion.
ca. 357	Dion seizes power in Syracuse from Dionysius but is assassinated three years later. Critics reproach Plato for his association with the tyrants Dion and Dionysius.
ca. 348	Plato dies in Athens and comes to be honored with the epithet "divine." He leaves behind 35 dialogues, all of which are preserved for posterity in the library of the Academy.

LITERARY AND HISTORICAL CONTEXT

1

Plato's Athens

THE ATHENIAN AGON

"The unexamined life is not worth living for a human being."[1] These words, uttered by Socrates as a reproach to the jurors at his trial, encapsulate two remarkable characteristics of Athenian public discourse in the fifth century B.C.: its persistent exploration of human experience, and its intense concentration on the problem of identifying the best life. Plato's *Republic* is a monumental example of precisely these concerns—specifically, of the philosophical investigation of human nature and the sources of worth and meaning in human life. Yet Plato's dialogues were fourth-century latecomers to an arena of public discourse that included the tragedies and satyr-plays of Aeschylus, Sophocles, and Euripides; the comedies of Aristophanes; the political orations of Pericles; the victory odes of Pindar; and the histories of Herodotus and Thucydides. Like all aspects of Greek public life since at least the time of Homer, this arena was structured as an agon, or competition. Just as athletes, playwrights, actors, and choruses competed for prizes at the many Athenian and Panhellenic festivals, all of the distinct voices and styles of speech just mentioned presented competing visions of the human lot—specifically, of the best human life in its relation to political community, to the gods, and to the cosmos. This agon was significant both philosophically and politically, since in the broadest terms the prize sought was wisdom—theoretical and practical knowledge of the whole of things, including both what is and what is best.

The Athenian quest for wisdom took place within the horizons of tradition, but the fifth-century Athenians understood the traditional conceptions of man and the world to be both flexible and open to interrogation. The status and nature of the gods is a case in point. Greek political communities were bound together by shared religious myths and rituals—stories about the gods and practices of religious observance—that placed Zeus and the pantheon of Olympian deities at the center of the divine realm.[2] Yet Socrates and his contemporaries were sensitive to the role of human interpretation in shaping the religious tradition; what is more, they were centrally concerned with the ambiguous status of the gods and the cosmic order they ostensibly represented and administered. According to the fifth-century historian Herodotus, chronicler of the wars between the Persian empire and the cities of Greece, the divine realm was disclosed for the Greeks by the poet Hesiod in the *Theogony* and by Homer in the *Iliad* and *Odyssey*: "Whence the gods severally sprang, whether or not they had all existed from eternity, what forms they bore—these are questions of which the Greeks knew nothing until the other day, so to speak. For Homer and Hesiod were the first to compose genealogies and give the gods their epithets, to allot them their several offices and occupations, and describe their forms; and they lived but 400 years before my time, as I believe."[3]

The Greek dramatists, in turn, were fully aware of even the most radical implications of Herodotus's remark: in Athens around the time of Plato's birth, for example, it was perfectly plausible for the character of Talthybius in Euripides' *Hecuba* to question whether the gods exist at all, and for the character of Socrates in Aristophanes' *Clouds* to assert that Zeus is a fiction.[4] Yet the plays of the Athenian dramatists were performed on sanctified grounds, at civic festivals held in honor of, and under the auspices of, the god Dionysus. In general, Athenian thought was remarkable in its simultaneous respect for, and inclination to examine critically, its traditional origins.

THE POLIS

The public debate just described owed its vitality to the polis, or city-state, the form of community from which we derive our word "political" and that is reflected in the title of Plato's *Politeia* (*Republic*). Greece in the time of Plato was not a united political entity, much less a nation-state of the sort with which we moderns are familiar. We must instead speak of a people, the Greeks, who lived in hundreds of politically independent communities (*poleis*) over an area stretching from the coasts of Spain and France to the eastern shores of the Aegean Sea and from the Black Sea to Libya but who were nonetheless bound together by a common language, by religious and literary tradition, and by political heritage.

Many *poleis* had fewer than 5,000 citizens. All citizens of the polis were adult males, but the community as a whole included slaves (typically captured in war) as well as resident alien businessmen. Athens, at the upper limit of *poleis* in size, had perhaps 25,000 citizens at the outbreak of the Peloponnesian War. Athens encompassed the entire region of Attica, within which lived perhaps 300,000 people (including women, children, resident aliens and slaves) when the war began. Geographically, the polis consisted of a walled town built around a hill or acropolis ("high polis") for defense and surrounded by farmland sufficient to sustain its members. Not everyone lived in the town, but all would seek refuge within its walls when the land was invaded by enemies.

The Greeks were most proud of the free and independent way of life they enjoyed in the polis.[5] The Greeks identified freedom with the rule of law, to which all citizens were equally subject. "Instead of living among barbarians," Jason reminds Medea in the course of listing the ways in which she has benefited from her association with him, "you inhabit a Greek land and know justice, and how to live by laws, not by the grace of force" (Euripides, *Medea*, 536-38). Neighbors who did not speak Greek were called *barbaroi*, apparently because foreign tongues sounded to the Greek ear like babble ("bar-barbar . . ."). There is a subtle political point beneath the apparent xenophobia of the term *barbarian*. To the Greeks, the greatest benefit of the rule of law was the opportunity it gave men to share in open public debate. Within the polis the individual citizen's logos—the word means both "speech" and "reason"; hence it is often best translated as "reasonable speech"—counted in the life of the community as a whole. The speech of the subjugated barbarian, however, was politically equivalent to babble, since it had no public significance. It is no accident that Jason immediately adds to his observation about the rule of law a further point about the honor that is available to the Greeks through logos: "If you were living at the ends of the earth, nobody would have heard of you"—literally, "there would have been no logos of you" (*Medea*, 540-41).

In sum, a Persian or an Egyptian lived an unenviable life because he inhabited an immense empire ruled by a despotic king. He was a subject, not a citizen. He was ruled but never took his turn at rule. Most important, what he said or did simply did not matter in the realm of politics. He was in every respect a very small fish in a very big pond. The polis, on the other hand, was a small pond, in which any citizen with ability in the affairs of war or peace could be a big fish. Indeed, this opportunity to stand out among one's peers was the driving force of public life in the polis. "This is the call of freedom," Theseus says in one tragic drama. "'What man has good advice to give the city, and wishes to make it known?' He who responds gains glory; the unwilling may hold their peace. For the city [polis], what can be more fair than that?" (Euripides, *Suppliant Women*, 438-41). Politically, the polis might be an aristocracy, oligarchy, or democracy, with intermittent episodes of tyranny. Whatever the form of its regime, however, the polis was a community that demanded the direct participation of its citizens in the affairs of war and peace.

The pride of the Athenians in their polis is perhaps best expressed in the famous oration of Pericles at the funeral of the first

Athenians killed in the Peloponnesian War.[6] According to Pericles, the polis alone makes possible a life truly worth living, for it alone allows the individual to make a difference in regard to truly noble and worthwhile issues. Indeed, our modern distinction between society, the broad realm within which individuals pursue private ends through public interactions, and politics, the much narrower sphere of government that protects and maintains society, implies a judgment about the relative value of private and public life that was quite foreign to the polis. "An Athenian citizen does not neglect the polis because he takes care of his own household," Pericles says in his funeral oration. "We alone regard a man who takes no interest in public affairs, not as a harmless, but as a useless character" (Thucydides, 2.40).

Plato's student Aristotle held a similar view. Aristotle maintained that the polis comes into being for the sake of mere life but continues in existence for the sake of the good life. Political community is constituted by our shared perceptions, articulated through logos, of the advantageous and the disadvantageous, the good and the bad, and the just and the unjust.[7] The seriousness and dignity of political life is derived from the seriousness and dignity of these political things, which have no equivalents in private life. Accordingly, the private man who shunned participation in public affairs was thought to be confused about the most important things: the Greeks called him an *idiōtēs*, from which comes our word *idiot*.

THE PROBLEM OF EXCELLENCE

While a shared sense of the importance of political life energized and ennobled public discourse, the participants in this discourse were well aware of certain fundamental tensions inherent in the souls of politicized human beings. These tensions expressed themselves in the violent history of the Greek cities, particularly Athens. The hostility generated by Athenian imperialism led eventually to the Peloponnesian War, which raged throughout Plato's childhood, youth, and early manhood.

In reviewing the story of the war and the lives of such outstanding Athenians of the age as Alcibiades, we may isolate two closely related problems at the roots of Greek public life.[8] First, the love of honor or glory—the passion that moved citizens of the polis to excel in public affairs—leads naturally to rivalry and war, both with other communities and within one's own community. The love of honor breeds jealousy of the great on the part of the small, and it breeds war because the man or city obsessed with glory tends to become tyrannical. Ultimately, the passion that sustains the community of honor lovers threatens also to destroy it: while the love of honor is closely linked with the virtues that contribute to good citizenship, in its extreme form it corrupts both the city and the soul. It is no accident that the foundational text of the Greek political tradition, Homer's *Iliad*, is essentially an exploration of precisely this issue.

Second, the love of honor is linked also with selfish appetites that oppose the development of public virtue. In the *Nicomachean Ethics* Aristotle initially claims that "men seem to pursue honor to assure themselves of their own worth; at any rate, they seek to be honored by sensible men and by those who know them, and they want to be honored on the basis of their virtue or excellence." But Aristotle later asserts that most men enjoy honor not because it confirms their own excellence but because it raises their hopes of obtaining benefits from people in positions of power.[9] In other words, most men are attracted to honor because it is a token of power, and power helps to guarantee the fulfillment of their appetites for pleasure and wealth.

Plato was deeply concerned with the challenges to human excellence posed by these selfish appetites. During the late fifth century, itinerant instructors known as sophists began to make money in Athens by teaching the art of rhetoric, which was useful to men seeking success in law and politics. Some sophists also attempted to legitimize the politically questionable deceptions of rhetoric by setting forth arguments that were intended to undermine the authority of law and custom and the claims of justice and that were sometimes used to defend the superiority of the life of unbridled hedonism. The growing importance of such arguments within the arena of public discourse may be gauged by their appearance in contemporaneous works such as

Euripides' *Cyclops*, a Homerically inspired satyr-play in which the Cyclops Polyphemus—a monster who lives alone, despises the gods, and eats visitors to his island cave—argues that might alone makes right, that the good life consists in indulging one's bodily appetites, and that "wealth [not Zeus] is god to the wise" (*Cyclops*, 316).

For Plato, the Cyclopean interpretation of human life that is rooted in the persistent claims of our bodily appetites constitutes a serious obstacle to the flourishing of both political community and philosophy. Yet philosophy and political community seem to stand in tension with one another as well as with our private, corporeal appetites, insofar as the acquisition of honor is no guarantee of genuine excellence. Because of its connection with the *desire* for excellence, however, the love of honor may be fertile soil in which to cultivate the love of human excellence for its own sake. In the *Republic* Socrates explores precisely this possibility in attempting to turn the political ambition of Glaucon away from the many pleasures of power and toward the achievement of excellence through philosophy.

2

The *Republic* and the Origins of Political Philosophy

Three hundred and fifty years after the death of Socrates, the Roman author Cicero recollected that Plato's teacher "was the first to call philosophy down from the heavens and set her in the cities of men, and bring her also into their homes, and compel her to ask questions about life and morality and things good and evil."[1] As Cicero points out, Greek philosophers prior to Socrates (the so-called pre-Socratics), unlike the Greek poets and historians, were more interested in investigating nature or "the heavens" than inquiring into human life. Socrates, however, turned the focus of philosophy away from inanimate nature and toward human things and thus radically transformed the nature of philosophy itself. He made philosophizing a public, political affair by actively questioning his fellow citizens about "life and morality and things good and evil." In calling philosophy down from the heavens and setting her in the cities of men, Socrates founded political philosophy (where "political" refers, in its broadest sense, to everything having to do with life in a human community).

Because Socrates left no writings, our most direct access to the original constellation of fundamental issues brought to light by political philosophy is through the works of Plato, which Plato once described as the writings "of a Socrates grown beautiful and young" (*Second Letter*, 314c1-4). As this quotation makes clear, the character of Socrates in the Platonic dialogues is not identical with the Socrates who actually lived and died in Athens, nor was Plato a mere scribe for the historical Socrates. In this connection, one commentator observes that "even if we make the most unintelligent assumption which, as it happens, is the most cautious assumption, that for all we know the Platonic dialogues might be verbatim reports of conversations, the selection of these particular 35 conversations would still be the work of Plato; . . . [for example,] Socrates must have had some conversations with Plato himself, and there is no Platonic dialogue in which Socrates converses with Plato."[2]

This is by no means to say that Plato's writings bear no relation to the historical Socrates or his political philosophizing. After all, the protagonist and indeed the hero of the dialogues is a character named Socrates.[3] In identifying his philosophic hero with "a Socrates grown beautiful and young," Plato indicates that what the dialogues present to us as philosophy is an *interpretation* of the philosophic activity of his own teacher. In short, Plato identifies philosophy with Socratic philosophizing, properly understood (and thereby purged of elements that are somehow "old" and "ugly"). The dialogues are vehicles for the preservation and transmission of this understanding.

Perhaps the most basic philosophical question with which Plato confronts his readers is, "What is Socratic philosophizing?" The *Republic*, Plato's most well-known dialogue, addresses this question in a comprehensive fashion. While all of Plato's writings are in some way concerned with Socrates' introduction of philosophy into the polis, the special importance of this topic within the *Republic* may be gauged from the dialogue's explicitly political theme, from the fact that Socrates is both its narrator and its protagonist, and from its plot or plan. Only two other Platonic works, the *Laws* and the *Statesman*, have titles that announce political themes; the *Laws*, in which Socrates does not appear, is also the only dialogue that is longer than the *Republic*. Besides the *Republic*, Socrates narrates just three other dialogues from beginning to end: the *Lovers, Charmides*, and *Lysis*.

Finally, the drama of the *Republic* in some sense reenacts the Socratic inauguration of political philosophy: Socrates spends all night introducing philosophy to a group of politically ambitious young men, defending it against their criticisms, and seducing them with its charms.

Among all of Plato's dialogues, the *Republic* brings us closest to the origins of political philosophy. This is the main reason for its enduring importance. Issues are frequently most broadly visible—and questions most profoundly posed—at the inception of an intellectual tradition, when prior teachings or theories cannot easily be taken for granted and common experiences and opinions are especially open to reexamination. The Greek *political* tradition, we should note, was also young in the days of Socrates: before Socrates' birth the polis had been in existence for only a few hundred years, and Athens had been democratic for less than half a century. With Socrates, philosophy becomes "political" both in its style (public questioning) and its focus (the human realm). Plato's *Republic* thus stands near the beginning of philosophy's primary concern with human life, as well as the initial entry of philosophy into the arena of public discourse about human affairs and the human lot. For these reasons modern readers continue to find that the *Republic* reopens, in fresh and provocative ways, the deepest questions about the human soul, human community, the proper objects of worship and reverence, the nature of philosophy, and the relationship between the philosopher and his political community.

3

Critical Provocations

The philosopher Alfred North Whitehead once observed that "the safest general characterization of the European philosophical tradition is that it consists of a series of footnotes to Plato."[1] It is at least as safe to construe the history of political philosophy as a series of responses to the *Republic*.

PROLOGUE: ARISTOPHANES' CONDEMNATION OF SOCRATES

The *Clouds* of Aristophanes (ca. 448-385 B.C.), a comic drama, was produced at Athens in 423 B.C. Its topic is Socrates—more specifically, the danger posed by Socratic philosophizing to the humanity of the Athenians and the integrity of their political community. Aristophanes depicts Socrates as the head of the *Phrontistērion*—"Thinketeria"—a place for the production of "new and strange" thoughts (*Clouds*, 896). The latter phrase anticipates the language of the indictment of 399 B.C., which charged Socrates with introducing "new and strange divinities." Indeed, the most significant of Socrates' novel thoughts in

13

the *Clouds* have to do with the gods. Specifically, Socrates denies the divinity of Zeus and refuses to acknowledge oaths sworn in the name of the Athenian gods (*Clouds*, 367, 247-48). Furthermore, Socrates' inclusion of Tongue among the list of the gods he acknowledges suggests that he views the gods as purely rhetorical entities (*Clouds*, 423).

Aristophanes connects Socrates' subversion of traditional religion with his wholesale perversion of justice and, more broadly, of the various human relationships by which political community is sustained. Socrates teaches the old man Strepsiades to cheat his creditors, because he learns that he can violate sworn oaths with impunity, but he also teaches Strepsiades' son that father-beating is acceptable, for Zeus *patrōon* ("Zeus, the protector of fathers") is a fiction (*Clouds*, 1468-71). In general, Socrates debunks the claim of logos to bind human beings together by articulating a common perception of the just, the good, and the noble: speech about these things, far from communicating shared standards of worth, ultimately reflects only the personal, private, fundamentally bodily appetites of the speaker. Strepsiades anticipates this teaching when, at the outset of the play, he compares the farts and snores of sleeping men to the debate by which the Athenian Assembly reaches a resolution (*Clouds*, 5-11).

Socrates first appears on stage suspended in a basket and contemplating the heavens, in which he sees not gods but merely physical nature (*Clouds*, 218). Socrates' elevation is metaphorically appropriate, since he consistently despises or looks down on human things as well as the gods (*Clouds*, 226, 1399-1400). The Thinketeria is depicted as a dark, vermin-filled, topsy-turvy world. While Socrates studies the heavens from his basket, his students are busy delving into the underworld, "with the anus looking at the heaven" and learning astronomy on its own (*Clouds*, 192-94). Just as the anus now does the work of the eye, Socrates' teaching fails to recognize the place of the divine things in the cosmos and thereby to differentiate between the high and the low. In addition, Socrates is equally concerned with tracing the great motions of the heavenly bodies and measuring the infinitesimal motions of fleas and gnats, but no one in the Thinketeria takes a theoretical interest in the things that are human in scale and place, the things that stand in between the high, heavenly realm and the low domain of animals and insects (*Clouds*, 144-72).

Without due attention to the human, middle ground, Aristophanes suggests, the high and the low become indistinguishable, and both the human and the divine things are debased. In ignoring that which elevates human beings above animals—a point underscored by abundant references to dogs and chickens (*Clouds*, 3, 491, 660-67, 810, 847-51, 1427-31; cf. 226)—Socrates' teaching perverts our experience of the sacred: his thoughts concerning the locomotion of fleas and the farts of gnats are described as "Mysteries," the word used for rites of religious initiation (*Clouds*, 143; cf. 250*ff*). And whereas religious initiation is supposedly a source of well-being, Socratic initiation actually harms the soul. The bonds of affection and friendship are absent from the Socratic universe: Socrates is a harsh master to his students, whose condition resembles that of captive, ill-treated beasts (*Clouds*, 184-86). Furthermore, Strepsiades likens the Thinketeria to a cave that was thought to lead down into the underworld, and he implicitly compares Socrates' "half-dead" students to the shades in Hades (*Clouds*, 504, 508; cf. 103, 119-20).

At his public trial, Socrates called Aristophanes the most influential of his "first accusers" (Plato, *Apology*, 18b-e). Aristophanes' accusation, like the later, official indictment, amounts to the charge that Socratic philosophizing is in fact a form of sophistry, understood as the sort of merely apparent wisdom that corrupts political community by undermining the traditional foundations of justice and friendship—especially religious reverence and awe—while putting nothing in their place.

To the jurors at his trial, Socrates' association with Alcibiades in particular must have seemed to confirm the claims of both his old and new accusers. Socrates claims in Plato's *Phaedo* that he was initially preoccupied with physical investigations (97b-100a), and it may be that the historical Socrates' turned away from pre-Socratic concerns and toward the human realm after the *Clouds* was first produced. Yet in important respects Aristophanes' accusation anticipates the criticisms of Aristotle and Nietzsche. Especially in the light of later responses to the dialogues, the *Clouds* forces readers of the *Republic* to ask why Aristophanes' and Athens's indictments of Socrates seemed plausible, and whether Socratic philosophizing can overcome the twin charge of bad theorizing and bad citizenship.

INTERPRETING EXTREMISM: ARISTOTLE
AND POPPER

Certain post-Platonic authors turned against the *Republic* the same sorts of charges Aristophanes leveled against Socrates. In particular, Plato's student Aristotle (384-22 B.C.) and the twentieth-century philosopher Karl Popper read the *Republic* as advocating a dangerous kind of political and philosophical extremism.

In the *Republic* Socrates and his companions attempt to construct a just "city-in-speech" in order to illustrate the nature of justice, by analogy, in the human soul (369a).[2] This process actually involves the successive construction of four separate cities: the City of Pigs and Feverish City of book 2 (369b-372d, 372e-374a); the City of Adeimantus, which is completed in book 4; and the Kallipolis, or "Noble and Beautiful City," which is finished in book 7. In book 5 Socrates introduces into the discussion of the just regime three "waves" of paradoxical political measures (457b-c, 472a). The regime requires that women and men engage in all pursuits in common, and that men hold women and children in common instead of forming separate families. Furthermore, Socrates asserts that cities will never rest from ills unless philosophers become kings or kings philosophers (473c-e).

Aristotle uses the notion of a practical pattern or blueprint in criticizing the communism of the Kallipolis. Socrates introduces the community of women and children in order to increase the unity of this city: without knowledge to the contrary, he argues, citizens would be inclined to regard one another as close family members. Aristotle, however, asserts that this measure would actually loosen the ties of friendship and justice that bind together members of a community. Possessing a thousand "children" or a thousand "parents," he maintains, would dilute the affection one feels for any particular person; in addition, such an arrangement would result in incest and other impieties. The city is in any case not a genuine community, for its army of Auxiliaries (414b) resembles an alien garrison camped within its borders (*Politics*, 2.2-5). Finally, Aristotle argues that the best regime would not be a philosophic monarchy but would instead provide all citizens with an opportunity to rule as well as to be ruled (*Politics*, 7.14).

Like many later critics, Aristotle implicitly assumes that Socrates' presentation of the Kallipolis is intended to provide human beings with a blueprint or ideal pattern for the organization of political communities, at least insofar as we are meant to understand that the Kallipolis would be the best of cities if it were actually to come into being. If one makes this assumption, the *Republic* advances a specific political program, and whatever is problematic or extreme in the Kallipolis will reflect the extremism or foolishness of Plato's politics.

Popper's work constitutes perhaps the most important example of the latter interpretive approach. In *The Open Society and Its Enemies* Popper argues that Plato was a proto-totalitarian whose anti-democratic writings continue to be politically "poisonous."[3] To support this thesis, Popper turns in particular to the *Republic*. The *Republic*, he claims, "was meant by its author not so much as a theoretical treatise, but as a topical political manifesto" whose ultimate aim was the establishment of a state identified with a racially superior ruling caste, supported by infanticide, censorship, and lies, and made possible by the "liquidation" of all political opposition (Popper, 1:153, 166; cf. 45-54). Plato's conception of justice is totalitarian, hence unjust; true justice is equalitarian. Likewise, Plato's society is closed, whereas the best society is "open"—that is, a society "in which individuals are confronted with personal decisions" (Popper, 1:86*ff*, 173).

The criticisms of Aristotle and Popper are valuable in that they call attention to the manipulative and prima facie unjust aspects of the Kallipolis. Furthermore, Popper's response to Plato underscores the extent to which the Kallipolis challenges our own equalitarian, democratic conceptions of justice. Socrates stresses, for example, the political instrumentality of religious mythology within the just city. This political use of poetry is rooted in the perception that fundamental differences between the moral and intellectual capabilities of the philosophic few and the nonphilosophic many justify lying. In particular, it seems to presuppose the impossibility of universal enlightenment while implicitly criticizing all regimes based on claims to rule other than wisdom.

In fine, Socrates strongly challenges our modern attachment to self-determination in constructing the city-in-speech. But it does not necessarily follow that Socrates, let alone Plato, wants the Kallipolis to be interpreted as a political blueprint or plan of action: perhaps Socrates is well aware of the deficiencies of this particular regime. Our ultimate assessment of the *Republic* will depend in part on whether we agree with Aristotle and Popper on this point. Let it suffice for now to note that our reading will explore and defend an alternative interpretive strategy.

FROM COSMOS TO CHAOS: NIETZSCHE

The Greek word *kosmos* means "ordered whole." Although the early modern philosophers replaced prior conceptions of the cosmos with the notion of an all-embracing physical system, it was still possible to speak of the world as an intrinsically ordered whole, albeit one in which the status of the moral and intellectual capabilities that seem most distinctively human became radically problematic. Friedrich Nietzsche (1844-1900), however, called into question even this attenuated notion of the cosmos. In so doing, he challenged Socratic philosophizing in a way that reiterates and extends the charges of Aristophanes.

Nietzsche in various places claims that all conceptions of order, and all human horizons, are constructions out of chaos. The world is a chaotic stream of ceaseless change, behind or beyond which there is no stable, enduring reality. There is consequently no truth independent of human perceptions; there are only perspectives that impose themselves on flux. All perspectives, in turn, originate in the chaotic war of drives or instincts; we interpret our experience in accordance with the drive that proves strongest. "Reason" too is a perspective. It is the name philosophers and scientists unwittingly give to their own dominant drives: "Every great philosophy so far has been . . . the personal confession of its author, and a kind of involuntary and unconscious memoir."[4]

In an early work Nietzsche argues at length that life is in itself oppressively meaningless. It becomes worth living not when it is philosophically examined, as Socrates had hoped, but only when it is "enhanced" by creative vision. Creative genius, however, can grow and ripen only in an atmosphere of illusion, and specifically only within the nurturing horizons of a culture, which present themselves as though they were the truth and thus mask the enervating meaninglessness of life.[5] The most important creations are thus those of the founders of cultures, whose comprehensive poetic vision brings order out of chaos. The highest human beings and greatest legislators are artists like Homer, not philosophers.

Nietzsche in fact challenges Socratic philosophizing to distinguish itself from poetry, understood as the creation of works of fiction as opposed to the discovery of truth. Whereas Socrates asserts that there is "an ancient quarrel between philosophy and poetry" (607b), Nietzsche argues in *The Birth of Tragedy* that the Platonic dialogues, at least insofar as they are formed "under the pressure of the demonic Socrates," are in effect bad poetry.[6] According to Nietzsche, Homer's "naive" poems represent the complete triumph over chaos of the illusion of order and harmony; they enhance life through the simplicity and beauty of their dreamlike images. The tragic dramas of Aeschylus and Sophocles enhance life in a different way: they submit to the inevitable dissolution of apparent order and yet in some measure overcome the suffering inherent in disorder, drawing strength from both the intoxication of chaos (the "Dionysian" impulse) and the healing power of poetic images (the "Apollonian" impulse). In the Platonic dialogues, as in Homer, the Apollonian dream of order banishes chaos. Yet Nietzsche maintains that Socrates saps the potentially life-enhancing power of this dream by confining the Apollonian impulse that graced Homer's naive art to "the cocoon of logical schematism" (Nietzsche 1967, 91) and by insisting that unchanging, formal, philosophical "truth"—which, as Socrates fails to see, is itself a fiction—is superior to poetry.

Finally, Nietzsche asserts that Socratic philosophizing is life-opposing, not life-enhancing. In a late work he claims that Socrates represented a kind of psychic sickness characterized by the tyranny of reason over the instincts.[7] Perhaps more important, Nietzsche, like Aristophanes, implicitly charges Socrates with diminishing human life by contributing to the destruction of political and cultural horizons.

Socratic inquiry begins by exposing the inadequacy of our convention-al or prephilosophical self-understanding in order to provoke investigation into the ultimate foundations of human life. Such inquiry understands itself to be engaged in the discovery of truth but overlooks the perspectival character of human experience. As a result, Socratic philosophizing is purely and profoundly destructive: it dismantles the merely apparent order of humanly manufactured custom or convention but is necessarily incapable of rediscovering order on the intrinsically chaotic and incoherent level of nature. Most important, cultural horizons themselves are always susceptible to being undermined by Socratic inquiry, which inevitably succeeds in exposing their unfounded character.

CONTEMPORARY CRITICISM: NUSSBAUM

One of the most important recent studies of Plato is Martha Nussbaum's *The Fragility of Goodness*.[8] While others working within the mainstream of Anglo-American Plato scholarship tend to discount the philosophic significance of Plato's literary style, Nussbaum insists that the dialogue form is essential to Plato's conception of teaching and learning. Like Nietzsche, Nussbaum believes that the full meaning of the dialogues can be appreciated only by viewing them in connection with the literary genre to which they are most closely related: Greek tragedy. Also like Nietzsche, Nussbaum considers the dialogues to be an "antitragic" response to tragic drama.

According to Nussbaum, tragedy recognizes that characteristically human attachments—especially those complex emotional ties that bind us to particular human beings through love, kinship, friendship, and the like—are intrinsically vulnerable to the vicissitudes of fortune and open to psychological and moral conflict and contradiction. Since such attachments, however, are essential to human goodness, human goodness is "fragile." While Nussbaum is prepared to accept the fragility of goodness, and even to find value in its fragility, she argues that Plato is not. In particular, she asserts that in the *Republic* Socrates identifies philosophy with the quest for goodness without fragility in the senses just described—a quest that involves transforming the soul so as to be able to dissolve one's attachments to all but purely intellectual ends and activities (Nussbaum, 90, 158-59).

The latter insight leads Nussbaum to formulate a criticism of Plato that in certain respects echoes the views of both Aristophanes and Nietzsche: the philosopher who attempts to overcome the tragic character of human existence learns thereby to despise that which is distinctively human, including just those features of life in human community that are celebrated in poetry because of their capacity to enhance and redeem our experience. In brief, Plato argues in the *Republic* for a superhuman life that is in certain ways less than human, because it is purchased by closing oneself off from many of the desires and emotions through which humanity is both learned and manifested (Nussbaum, 160).

PERVASIVE CRITICAL THEMES

Critics of the *Republic* consistently return to the problem of the tension between Socratic philosophy and essential features of human experience, including in particular the modes of thought and life that sustain political community. This problem, which turns on the relationship between *phusis* ("nature") and *nomos* ("custom," "convention," or "law"), assumes several forms. Aristophanes suggests that it is in the nature of Socratic philosophizing to dissolve the bonds of *nomos* and thereby to corrupt political community, insofar as *phusis* alone cannot support human political existence. Nietzsche develops a similar argument about the destructive effect of philosophic inquiry on cultural horizons, and therefore on the individual human beings who find shelter within these horizons. Whatever Aristophanes' understanding of *phusis* may be—and his thought on this matter seems in important respects to resemble Nietzsche's—he indicates that Socratic investigation leaves one with a harsh and godless conception of the cosmos that is incompatible with the aspirations, hopes, and fears that sustain both the polis and its individual members.

Aristotle—who was himself ultimately charged with impiety by the Athenians—is more moderate in his criticism: like Popper, he does not find fault with Socratic inquiry per se but with what he takes to be the Platonic political program. Aristotle and Popper call our attention to issues of textual interpretation, to the extreme character of the Kallipolis, and to substantive questions about the theoretical presuppositions of democratic equalitarianism. Nussbaum accepts the classical understanding of political philosophy as a quest for knowledge of the good but finds in the *Republic* a conception of philosophy that is defective insofar as it is closed to many of the sources of value in human life.

To answer Nietzsche, the *Republic* somehow has to show that Socratic, philosophic education is more than just a pipe dream and that philosophic logos is not just bad poetry. Beyond this, the *Republic* has to defend its author as well as its protagonist against the recurring accusations of deficient humanity and bad citizenship first formulated by Aristophanes. Even if philosophy is possible, is it desirable? Part of our task in examining the *Republic* is to show how the work itself poses and addresses this question with maximum clarity.[9]

A READING

4

Prelude: Interpreting Plato

One cannot understand Plato without paying due attention to his style. The first thing to notice about the dialogues is their unusual literary form, which may seem more suited to a stage play than to philosophic argument. This reading situates the *Republic* within the context of ancient Greek literature and uses interpretive strategies appropriate to literature because Plato *himself* evidently viewed the dialogues as a philosophical development of the Greek literary tradition. Why did Plato write dialogues, and in what relation does the *Republic* stand to other literary genres? These questions guide our interpretation of the *Republic*.

PLATO'S PHILOSOPHIC DRAMAS

Plato's contribution to the tradition of Athenian public discourse was marked by the combination of innovation and critical respect that had already come to characterize the tradition as a whole. Plato entered the arena of Athenian public discourse in a novel way. According to an ancient story, he wrote a dramatic tetralogy (three tragedies and a satyr-play) that he intended to place in competition at the City Dionysia but instead burned after an encounter with Socrates.[1] This anecdote may be fictitious, but it alerts us to the fact that Plato's writings in some sense constitute a philosophical appropriation and transformation of dramatic poetry.

One point of contact between Plato and the Athenian playwrights seems clear: just as the tragedians reconfigured as tragic protagonists the earlier heroes of Homeric epic, Plato invented a new literary genre, the dialogue or philosophic drama, and a new kind of literary hero, the philosopher. Like the tragic and satyric dramatists, Plato frequently borrows the images, myths, and even the plots of epic poetry. Yet the dialogues also resemble Aristophanic comedy in certain basic ways: they are set in fifth-century Athens, not in the remote mythical past; their characters are often likenesses of recognizable contemporaries of Socrates; and some of them, including the *Republic*, are full of laughter and laughable things.[2] The dialogues are thus both innovative and conservative: they incorporate elements of preexisting styles of public discourse while at the same time distinguish themselves from these literary styles as a new kind of discourse.

Why did Plato choose to go beyond the genres of tragedy, satyr-play, and comedy and still incorporate important elements of each genre in his work? If one supposes that the latter styles of discourse struck Plato as insufficiently philosophical, why did he not write treatises in the manner of the pre-Socratic philosophers Zeno and Gorgias?[3] An adequate answer to these questions must take into account the pedagogical advantages of the dialogue form as well as the philosophical meaning of Plato's adaptation of developed poetic genres. Let us consider each of these points in turn.

THE DIALOGUE AS TEACHER

Socrates was a reader but, with one exception, not a writer: shortly before his death he composed a hymn to Apollo and some versifications of Aesop's fables (*Phaedo*, 60c-61b). What is more, Socrates

opposed the practice of writing for pedagogical reasons. On one occasion he criticized the written word for being mute when questioned,
repetitive, unable to keep silence when it ought to, and unable to
defend itself against misinterpretation (Plato, *Phaedrus*, 275d-e).
Plato's decision to write, however, suggests that in his view the dialogue form captures some of the pedagogical advantages of live conversation.

While most works of philosophy are treatises in which the
author argues in his own voice in defense of some thesis, the dialogues
are dramas that present us with the speeches and deeds of characters
who are themselves engaged in philosophic debate. Plato never speaks
directly to his readers in the dialogues, and so he never directly tells us
what he thinks, or what we ought to think. The dialogues thus leave
the burden of interpretation to the reader, who must actively interro-
gate the text if he is to discriminate intelligently between the competing positions represented therein. In their provocative and open-ended
character, Plato's writings imitate Socrates' conversational style and
point toward his agreement with the Socratic principle that the teacher
should direct the learner toward the task of educating *himself* (cf.
Plato, *Theaetetus*, 149a-151d).

Because the dialogues combine the concrete texture of human
life with philosophical argument, they demand of their readers a poetic sensibility as well as logical acuity. Plato's writings are not arguments abstracted from their conversational contexts but embody these
rich contexts in the flesh and blood of human characters. Plato thus
keeps the reader's gaze fixed on the emergence of philosophical debate
from ordinary human experience. In so doing, he repeatedly reminds
the reader that philosophy is born from characteristically human
desires and concerns and that the meaning of philosophical arguments
cannot be severed from the activity of philosophizing as a way of life.
As we shall see, Plato's use of poetry in the *Republic* is designed to
reinforce these lessons.[4]

TRAGEDY AND COMEDY IN THE *REPUBLIC*: RETHINKING NUSSBAUM

The dramatic form of the dialogues links them with Greek tragedy. Socrates, the protagonist of most of Plato's philosophic plays, typically encounters self-confident antagonists and proceeds to show them that their seemingly sensible and consistent opinions turn out, on close scrutiny, to be deeply incoherent. Similarly, the characters of tragic drama typically stand in antagonistic relationships with one another and learn through a sequence of tragic events that their traditional or habitual assumptions about themselves and the world are woefully incapable of guiding them through the complexities and uncertainties of human experience. In its persistent exposure of the ambiguities and contradictions at the heart of human self-understanding, Greek tragedy is essentially philosophical, and indeed essentially Socratic.[5]

We must nonetheless read Plato's dialogues against a literary backdrop that includes more than tragic drama. Nussbaum notes that "Plato acknowledges the influence . . . of at least six different kinds of texts: epic, lyric, tragic, and comic poetry, the prose scientific or historical treatise, and oratory" (Nussbaum, 123). In her treatment of the *Republic*, however, she mentions neither comedy nor epic. Her silence about these matters is especially significant, for Socrates underscores certain laughable aspects of his own argument precisely in order to show that he takes seriously the accusations of the greatest of the comic dramatists—accusations that closely resemble Nussbaum's criticisms.

Despite Aristophanes' criticisms of Socrates, Plato evidently regarded the comic poet as a kindred spirit. He is said to have written the following epigram on the occasion of Aristophanes' death: "The Graces, seeking to grasp some sacred ground that would not fall, discovered the soul of Aristophanes."[6] Given these beautiful words, it is not surprising to find that the *Republic* is on one level a sophisticated and respectful response to the *Clouds*. Certain structural similarities support this interpretation. In both works Socrates "descends" (in one case from his basket to the ground, in the other from Athens to the Piraeus) to "initiate" nonphilosophers into the "Mysteries" of philosophy. Furthermore, both works center on the conflict between justice and injustice (personified in one case by the Just and the Unjust Speeches, in the other by Socrates and the pair of Thrasymachus and Glaucon). No less obvious are Socrates' allusions in book 5 to Aristophanes' *Assemblywomen* (392 B.C.), in which enduring political problems are addressed, as in the Kallipolis, by means of radical measures pertaining to the relations between women and men. In addition, Socrates' literal descent to the Piraeus and metaphorical "ascent" in speech to the Kallipolis are prefigured in two Aristophanean dramas: the *Frogs* (405 B.C.), in which Dionysus goes down to Hades and learns there about the political importance of poetry, and the *Birds* (414 B.C.), in which two Athenians, fleeing the hardships of life in Athens, become the founders of an "ideal" city in the sky: Cloud Cuckooland. More than one author, having noted the above comic parallels, has concluded that Plato wants indirectly to underscore the ugly and ridiculous character of the city Socrates ironically names "Noble and Beautiful."[7]

Like Popper, Nussbaum fails to appreciate Socratic irony: she takes seriously parts of Socrates' argument that he himself indicates are no less absurd than the comedies of Aristophanes. This failure is especially important because Nussbaum and Aristophanes both argue that Socrates becomes less than human in his attempt to transcend the merely human, and Aristophanes' indictment was already familiar to Plato when he wrote the *Republic*. Furthermore, Socrates alludes most frequently to Aristophanes and most emphasizes laughter precisely when his argument does the most violence to human things—specifically, when he introduces measures in book 5 that purge human sexual desire of the sacred and gracious elements of beauty, affection, and enchantment, in part by eliminating marriage and the family and instituting the breeding of human beings in pens like animals (cf. Saxenhouse, 897, 899). Plato's Socrates thus acknowledges in the course of constructing the Kallipolis that he is acting like Aristophanes' Socrates, whose irreverent and unjust speech effectively reduced men to beasts. In so doing, Socrates ironically undercuts and distances himself from some of the central elements of the very argument he sets forth.

One further aspect of Nussbaum's reading deserves mention here. Like most Plato scholars, Nussbaum assumes that we know roughly the order in which the dialogues were written, and that this information is crucial to understanding Plato's thought. Yet as has recently been shown elsewhere, neither of these widely held assumptions is well-founded, and both are beset with serious difficulties. The ancient evidence suggests that Plato viewed his dialogues not as an unfolding sequence of more or less mature philosophical positions but as a kind of literary cosmos held together by a variety of dramatic and thematic devices.[8]

It is often helpful to consider features of the *Republic* in light of other dialogues that are conventionally regarded as belonging to "earlier" or "later" periods of Plato's philosophical career—a procedure that orthodox assumptions about chronology would render illegitimate. Insofar as the latter assumptions are themselves unwarranted, however, we should not be surprised to find that the *Republic* is far more compatible than Nussbaum suspects with ostensibly "later" dialogues like *Phaedrus* (cf. Nussbaum, 228).

EPIC: PLATO'S ADAPTATION OF HOMER

Plato's use of Homeric imagery in the *Republic* is no less important than his responsive dialogue with Aristophanes and the tragic dramatists. In an article that explores the connections between Homeric mythology and the *Republic*, Charles Segal manages to illuminate Plato's reasons for using poetic language in general.[9] Segal notes that in the *Republic* Plato shares Homer's aim of comprehending the human condition within "a large, unifying vision of reality." In order to do so, Plato, like Homer, must use "the patterns crystallized by an ancient mythical tradition" (Segal 1978, 316). In support of this claim, Segal observes that myth is "the language of the adventures of the soul," "the educator of the soul's loves," and "a bridge between the darker and the more rational parts of our natures." Hence, while Plato's "vast enterprise of reeducating the human soul" leads him to undertake a fundamental transformation of the poetic tradition, "[Plato] still requires the hoary archetypes of myth, for it may be that only through myth and mythical images can the soul ultimately be known" (Segal 1978, 329*ff*).[10]

Perhaps most important, Plato models the philosopher after the pattern of the epic hero, who confronts "crisis, conflict, and tragic choice" and with "singleness of devotion" searches for "the meaning of human life in the face of death" (Segal 1978, 320-21, 322). Segal observes that in the *Republic* Plato makes use of ancient mythical archetypes to explore the self and the soul's "inward journey to perfection" in a way that parallels Homer's use of the same archetypes in recounting the homeward voyage of Odysseus (Segal 1978, 329*ff*). Yet Plato's adaptation of Homer is Socratically open-ended: "the new, philosophical 'epic' will explore, not codify or transmit; it claims epic seriousness and even heroic status for its material, but not the epic finality of a closed, perfected tradition" (Segal 1978, 325).

PLATO'S PHILOSOPHIC POETRY

Because the Platonic dialogue is not simply tragedy, comedy, or epic, it is able to exploit the virtues of each of these genres. Thus, although the *Republic* appropriates the mythical structure of Homeric epic in depicting the quest for wisdom, it does so in a way that incorporates tragic and comic sensibilities. The result is a specifically philosophical kind of drama that brings together the comprehensiveness and mythical profundity of epic quest, the antidogmatic openness and sense of paradox characteristic of tragedy, and the ironic detachment and critical self-awareness of comedy. In Plato's *Symposium* (223d) Socrates argues that the same author should be able to write both tragedy and comedy. In the same dialogue Alcibiades compares Socrates to the satyrs Silenus and Marsyas (*Symposium*, 215a*ff*). Perhaps the dialogues of Plato are closest of all to the dramatic form that typically brought tragedy and comedy to bear on epic themes: the satyr-play.

31

5

The Philosophic Odyssey

Unlike most philosophical classics, the *Republic* is a literary master-piece. As such, the *Republic* cannot be fully understood without appreciating the way in which its narrative, dramatic, and mythical elements reinforce one another in framing and developing the work's fundamental issues.

The *Republic*'s structure places special emphasis on the themes of philosophic recollection and philosophic *erōs*, or desire. These themes, in turn, are connected with the dramatic motif of ascent and descent that runs throughout the dialogue. Plato's use of this motif indicates that Socrates is the hero—and, as narrator, in a sense also the author—of a philosophic epic cast in the form of a philosophic drama. In particular, the homeward quest of Odysseus is woven into the dialogue as a mythical subtext of its philosophic action.[1] Lest this Homeric formulation sound too exalted, one should recall Aristotle's remark that the structure and peculiar pleasures of the *Odyssey* are characteristically comic, not tragic.[2] Similarly, while it is important to note that the structure of the *Republic* imitates that of initiation into the Mysteries, an originally tragic theme, we shall also trace the ways in which Plato, ironically mimicking Aristophanes, exposes Socrates' philosophic activity to ridicule.[3]

In book 2 Socrates tells Adeimantus that "the beginning is the most important part of every work" (377a). Plato appears to have followed this maxim in his own writing, because the dialogue begins in such a way as to alert us to its overarching structure. We therefore begin our reading by examining the ways in which the interrelated structural dimensions of the *Republic*—the dimensions of narrative, argument, drama, and myth—are embedded within and anticipated by its opening pages.

NARRATIVE, ARGUMENT, AND DRAMA

Recollection and Philosophic Comprehension   The *Republic* is narrated by Socrates for an unspecified audience on the day after the conversation recorded in it takes place. We do not view the action directly, for the dialogue we read is a recollected conversation that Socrates has mentally annotated and edited; he occasionally reveals some of his private thoughts, and in a few places he chooses to summarize, rather than to report in detail, what was said or done.

The narrative structure of the *Republic* thus emphasizes Socrates' appropriation of prior experience through recollection and calls attention to the steps he takes to cast this material into the unified form of a story. Socratic recollection, in other words, is neither passive nor piecemeal; it seeks actively to comprehend the internal coherence of experience. In the *Republic* narrative is the means by which Socrates articulates philosophic comprehension. The prodigious act of literal recollection by which Socrates preserves the dialogue for us anticipates the theme of "recollection" in an extended, philosophical sense.

At the end of the *Republic* (621b-d) Socrates retrospectively connects human salvation with the power of philosophic recollection. In particular, he urges his friends to remember the teaching of the Myth of Er he has just finished telling, a myth that depicts the philosophic quest for knowledge of the soul and the best life as a struggle against forgetfulness. The teaching with which the dialogue concludes thus points back to both Socrates' literal recollection of the conversation and the quest for self-knowledge that he and his companions have undertaken over the course of the evening. The dialogue's narrative structure underscores this point, for the *Republic* ends in direct discourse even though it began in indirect discourse. The effect is to make the reader forget that Socrates is narrating the dialogue. It is as though the past, having been "saved" (like Er's tale of the afterlife) by the power of recollection, were thereby rendered fully present.[4] Form and content join in a harmonious whole; as a paradigm of the various senses of recollection, the *Republic* dramatically enacts Socrates' teaching.

The narrative structure of the *Republic* suggests that the dialogue may provide the reader with a route to self-knowledge, to the extent that he is able retrospectively to bring together or "re-collect" the *Republic* as a whole and grasp it in its philosophic integrity. What would an "ideal" reading of the *Republic*—one that grasps the dialogue as a whole—look like? We begin to answer this question when we notice that Socrates recollects and narrates the evening's events in a richly detailed manner and does not limit himself merely to repeating the various arguments that were advanced over the course of the conversation. Socrates' narrative procedure suggests that to understand the *Republic* one must shuttle back and forth between drama and explicit argument. As in human life in general, the significance of *logos* (speech) becomes fully visible only in its relation to *ergon* (deed). But what is the *ergon* or accomplishment of the *Republic*?

Because the title of the dialogue prepares us for an inquiry into the nature of political community, what justifies the guiding assumption of this study—namely, that the primary aim of the *Republic* is to illuminate the origins, nature, and worth of philosophy? This chapter offers a preliminary response to this question; for now it suffices to anticipate two important points: (a) the construction of the Kallipolis—a city many have described as a closed, manipulative regime—takes place within the context of an unplanned, open-ended conversation; (b) the philosophic way of life embodied in and sustained through Socratic discourse differs strikingly from the kinds of lives possible in the Kallipolis, even for the philosopher-king. The tension between *logos* and *ergon* in the *Republic* suggests that its lessons concerning both philosophy and politics are not straightforwardly contained in Socrates' arguments concerning the Kallipolis but come to light only through reflection on the relation between the community of discourse that forms around him in the dialogue and the mythical community over which the philosopher-king presides.

The argumentative structure of the dialogue—the form and content of the inquiry—is embedded within its dramatic structure, whose elements include the *Republic*'s setting, its characters, and their deeds. Speaking and remaining silent, of course, are also important kinds of deeds. For this reason, it is perhaps best simply to describe the *Republic* as a philosophic drama, a designation intended to capture the unity of argument and drama within the activity of dialogue.

Erōs and the Origins of Philosophy

How does philosophy get started? How does the community of philosophic discourse that forms around Socrates come to be, and what sustains it throughout the night?[5] The opening scene of the *Republic* (327a-28b), which constitutes a prologue to the dialogue, raises the latter question by calling attention to the initial conflict between Socrates' philosophic desire and the more common appetites that bring his companions together. In addition, the prologue connects this conflict with the larger issue of the problematic relationship between the philosopher and political community. The action of the prologue thus provides us with the initially antagonistic context within which the philosophic discussion emerges.

On the day the *Republic* takes place, a new religious cult is being founded in the Piraeus—that of the Thracian (barbarian) goddess Bendis (354a). As Athens's seaport, the Piraeus was a center of commerce, the home of many foreign businessmen, and the point of entry for foreign influences of all sorts. There is no equivalent to the Piraeus in the just city-in-speech, whose rulers carefully guard against innovation in order to protect their political traditions from corruption (424b). The openness of Athens, however, seems to suit Socrates. Socrates tells us that he and Glaucon walked from Athens to the Piraeus to pray to the goddess—probably Bendis—and to observe the new religious festival. After they had prayed and looked on, they started back toward Athens (327a).

These first lines of the *Republic* sketch the character of the philosopher. The verb "to observe" is *theasthai*, "to behold with a sense of wonder." "Looked on" translates *theōrein*, "to look at, especially with the mind; to contemplate"; it is the root of our word *theory*. Like philosophy itself, Plato suggests, the *Republic* begins in a sense of wonder (cf. *Theaetetus*, 155d). Socrates is attracted by his sense of wonder toward the contemplation of a new religious festival. Furthermore, Socrates' contemplation or "theorizing" is not in any straightforward sense limited by patriotism: he maintains that the procession conducted by the Thracians was as good as that of the Athenians (327a). The philosopher's judgment evidently transcends the patriotic horizons of the good citizen and is thus potentially revolutionary.

The dialogue begins accidentally. Socrates makes it clear that he initially had no intention of remaining in the Piraeus. He and Glaucon would have made it home that night if they had not been spotted walking toward Athens by a group of young men, including Polemarchus and Glaucon's brother Adeimantus. Polemarchus, whose name means "War-Leader," peremptorily orders Socrates and Glaucon to wait and jokingly suggests that he and his friends will use force to keep them from leaving the Piraeus without joining them for dinner (327c). Besides, Adeimantus points out, there will be a torch-race on horseback and an all-night festival, and Polemarchus adds that they will all get together with many other young men and talk. Socrates is impressed by the novelty of the torch-race, and in any case Glaucon, who clearly wants to stay for the big party, flatly proclaims that he and Socrates must remain. "If it is so resolved," Socrates concedes, "that's how we must act." It is not yet clear why Socrates yields to his companions. In any case, the group then retires to the home of Polemarchus, where the conversation itself begins (328b).

The phrase "if it is so resolved" was used in the Athenian Assembly to signal the passage of a law. More important, at the beginning of Aristophanes' *Clouds* the insomniac character Strepsiades utters the same phrase in response to the bodily rumblings of his sleeping household—a joke that suggests that when human beings speak, they resemble sleeping men passing gas (*Clouds*, 11). Speech, in other words, is at bottom uncommunicative because it is purely self-serving; one could say that it is merely a means to relieve the pressure of our private, bodily desires. The present passage from the *Republic* is therefore provocatively ambiguous. On the surface, it seems to imply that Socrates and his companions form a miniature political community. Like political communities, this association originates in common needs and desires (in this case, the young men's appetite for food and drink, new amusements, and one anothers' society) and is initially held together by force (represented in the opening scene by the spirited pair of Polemarchus and Glaucon) and persuasion (represented by Adeimantus) in the service of these desires. On a deeper level, Plato's allusion to the *Clouds* challenges the claim of this or any other association to be a community at all, for genuine community (as opposed to a tenuous aggregate of individuals) presupposes logos—that is, reasonable speech capable of binding men together by means of its power to articulate the common good. The *Republic* thereby assumes the burden of showing that speech is more than the inarticulate and intrinsically noxious or combative noise of "sleeping" men, in that it is capable of pointing beyond the personal and private desires of the speaker and toward standards of worth that can potentially be shared by many.

Strepsiades' joke in the *Clouds* anticipates in particular the unjust speech of Socrates. The *Republic* will thus also have to answer Aristophanes' charge that philosophy is incompatible with, and indeed destructive of, just those traditional customs and convictions that hold the polis together. In this connection it is crucial to observe that the *Republic*'s prologue first acquaints us with the politically uninhibited character of philosophic wonder, and only then does it introduce the problem of the relationship between human beings in a political community. Our first view of politics in the *Republic*, in other words, is from the perspective of the mutual challenge posed by the philosophic way of life and the lives of the majority of nonphilosophers.

While the argument concerning the Kallipolis addresses this challenge, the *Republic* explores it dramatically as well. As noted, these two avenues of inquiry seem to conflict with each other. Unlike the Kallipolis, which is maintained not by the unifying power of logos but by military might and clever deceptions, a genuine community of discourse comes into being in the dialogue because of the shared philosophic *erōs* that begins to grow within its members. In recognizing this tension between the argument and action of the *Republic*, we begin to confront the deeply problematic character of *erōs*.

The root meaning of *erōs* is sexual desire; more broadly, *erōs* designates other kinds of passionate desires as well. Just as the depths of human sexual desire contain more than mere lust, so that *erōs* is often translated as "love," *erōs* in its distinctively human forms transcends mere appetite. *Erōs* is definitive of the human condition: it is not a specific, discrete desire of a part of the soul or body, like thirst, but a mysterious longing of body and soul as a whole for whatever it is that will provide us with comprehensive satisfaction. At its best, *erōs* is a gentle teacher; at its worst, it is a savage and tyrannical monster. In the *Symposium* (201d-12c) Socrates emphasizes the former aspect of *erōs* and offers an account of the transformation of sexual desire—the most primal passion and the first expression of man's longing for immortality—into philosophic *erōs*. In the *Republic*, Socrates acknowledges the ambiguity of *erōs*, which he associates especially with the tyrannical but also with the philosophical soul. Thus, while he emphasizes the need to control and contain *erōs* in the just city, he simultaneously provokes the *erōs* of his interlocutors through dialogue and attempts to channel it in the direction of philosophy.[6]

A synopsis of the action of the *Republic* will help us to appreciate the close connection between the problem of *erōs* and the relationship between argument and drama in the dialogue.

Overview of the *Republic* The conversation gets under way in the home of Polemarchus. Those present include both native Athenians (Socrates, Plato's brothers Glaucon and Adeimantus, Niceratus, Charmantides, and Cleitophon) and foreigners (the resident alien Cephalus and his sons Polemarchus, Lysias, and Euthydemus, and the sophist Thrasymachus). The aged Cephalus, who spent his most vital years gratifying a multiplicity of appetites as though he were the slave of "very many mad masters" (329d), embodies the withered aftermath of tyrannical *erōs*. Yet Cephalus does not regret his youth, although he fears punishment for the acts of injustice that followed from his desires. Injustice and erotic satisfaction are thus linked from the outset of the dialogue. What is more, Thrasymachus and Glaucon subsequently defend Cephalus's association of the gratification of tyrannical *erōs* with happiness, while attempting to liberate the life of injustice from the fears that plague Cephalus. The *Republic* quickly establishes its basic dramatic armature: Socrates must defend both philosophy and justice against the multifarious attractions of full-blown erotic liberty.

In book 1 Socrates meets the challenges of Polemarchus and Thrasymachus by showing these men that their speeches, far from refuting or silencing Socrates, implicate them in further philosophic inquiry. Having concluded the discussion he relates in book 1 Socrates tells us that "I thought I was freed from argument. But after all, as it seems, it was only a prelude" (357a). Plato's brothers now challenge Socrates to defend justice against an improved Thrasymachean argument for perfect injustice. Socrates' companions, it appears, have by this time forgotten about the torch-race and the festival; they have forgotten to eat as well and will even forget about sleeping this night. By giving free rein to speech about erotic satisfaction, Socrates has allowed philosophic desire to grow out of prephilosophical *erōs*. It is the *erōs* of his companions, sustained by their high spirits, that propels the conversation forward and subsumes in speech the passions that first brought them together.

In response to the challenges of Glaucon and Adeimantus, Socrates proposes in book 2 to found a just city-in-speech: perhaps the justice that comes to light in this city will clarify, by analogy, the nature of justice in the soul. Socrates soon proceeds to focus on the education of the Guardians of the just regime. This education, which is designed to minimize both models of, and opportunities for, the exercise of desires that may lead to injustice, involves both a radical revision of the existing poeticoreligious tradition and a strict regimen whereby good citizens are bred and trained like animals.

Socrates observes that in educating the Guardians he and his companions act "just as men mythologizing in a myth" (376d), a remark that simultaneously underscores Socrates' role as a dramatic character in a dialogue and the mythical character of the city-in-speech. Socrates proceeds to replace the old Hesiodic and Homeric myths about the gods with new myths suited to the production of just individuals. Human beings look up to and imitate their gods, but Socrates does not think that the Olympian gods, at least insofar as they are portrayed by the poets, are worthy of imitation. Unlike the Olympian gods, Socrates' new gods do not fight with one another, do not lie, are never overcome by laughter, never change shape, and are the cause of all good things for human beings, but of no bad things (377e-89a). In short, the new, unchanging gods of books 2 and 3 closely resemble the Ideas, the true "gods" of the philosopher that Socrates introduces in book 5.[7]

Like the Ideas, which are not alive, Socrates' new gods are altogether without *erōs*. For this reason they are excellent models of moderation for human beings. Yet Socrates' account of education is not consistent in regard to *erōs*: while justice demands the restriction of desire, Socrates acknowledges that education involves the provocation and seduction of *erōs* by that which is intrinsically beautiful: "musical matters should end in love matters [*erōtika*] that concern the beautiful and noble" (403c).

When Socrates reaches an appropriate stopping point at the end of book 3, Adeimantus protests that the city-in-speech would not make its citizens happy, and Adeimantus and his friends, being young, are especially concerned with the question of the happiest life. Socrates is therefore compelled in book 4 to defend the city he has constructed, a city he now identifies with Adeimantus (427c). His defense rests on the claim that this city, like the soul, is divided into three distinct parts— one characterized by "calculation" (*logismos*), one by "spiritedness" (*thumos*), and one by "appetite" (*epithumia*)—and that the virtues of each part and of the whole the parts form—wisdom, courage, moderation, and justice—are to be found in both the well-ordered city and the well-ordered soul. Socrates now confines *erōs* to the epithumetic element of the tripartite soul and city (439d), which implies that *erōs* is merely one appetite among many. Yet we should not be quick to accept any part of the argument of book 4, since Socrates indicates that the present conversation takes place in the intellectual equivalent of darkness (427d, 432d).

At the end of book 4 Socrates intends to proceed directly to a discussion of the city's decay. Yet he is again interrupted, this time by Polemarchus. Polemarchus and the others accuse Socrates of cheating them out of a whole section of the argument: they want to hear more about his claim that women and children should be held in common by the citizens of the just regime. Since it pertains to sex, Socrates' radical proposal would naturally arouse great interest among youthful males. Reluctantly and with trepidation (450a*ff*), Socrates launches into a digression that takes up books 5 through 7 and that includes in the images of the Sun, Line, and Cave an account of the Ideas, the Good, and the nature of philosophic education.

It seems that Socrates initially intended to ignore the topics of sex as well as philosophic rule in his discussion of the just regime. The City of Adeimantus, it must be stressed, is without philosophy: it is ruled by Guardians trained to cling to politically salutary "dogmas" (*dogmata*: 414b; cf. 412e, 413c). The hesitancy with which Socrates approaches the subject of philosophy arises in part from the tension and ambiguity within *erōs* itself, which manifests itself especially in the apparent conflict between justice and political community on the one hand and critical, philosophical thought on the other. In particular, it is not easy to reconcile the highly erotic nature of the philosopher (475c*ff*, 485b-e) with a simultaneous attack on *erōs* as a source of injustice and tyrannical enslavement, or with the educational dogmatism of both Adeimantus's city and the philosophical regime Socrates names "Kallipolis" and identifies with Glaucon (527c). Yet Socrates is compelled by the conflicted *erōs* of his companions, with its potent mixture of powerful appetites and sexual and philosophic longing, to attempt precisely such a reconciliation.

Only in book 8 does Socrates return to the theme he had intended to pursue after book 4: the unavoidable decay of the just regime. This degeneration results specifically from the impossibility of regulating *erōs* with technical or quasi-mathematical precision. Socrates' fantastically complicated explanation of the so-called Nuptial Number (546a-47a)—which he puts in the mouth of the Muses, who "speak to us with high tragic talk, as though they were speaking seriously, playing and jesting with us like children" (545e)—indicates that as a political blueprint the Kallipolis is no less ridiculous than its Aristophanean counterparts, and that to take it seriously as such is to fall victim to a Platonic joke.

In turning away from the laughable project of a philosophical regime, Socrates traces in books 8 and 9 the shifting interplay of psychological and political forces through which actual kinds of regimes and corresponding types of souls reciprocally determine one another. This discussion culminates in Socrates' description of the tyrant's soul and the depths of his misery, at which point Socrates has finally finished responding to the praise of tyranny set forth by Glaucon and Thrasymachus at the beginning of the dialogue. At the same time, the cycle of degeneration Socrates presents in books 8 and 9 leads to the conclusion that philosophy is a means of *individual* salvation only.

In book 10 Socrates returns to the topic of poetry, particularly tragedy, which he associates with the aforementioned corrupting forces. Yet he exploits the philosophical dimensions of tragedy by concluding the *Republic* with a tale that expresses the tragic paradoxes of human responsibility and self-knowledge. The Myth of Er is both a final plea for philosophical education and a metaphorical representation of the profound problems we encounter in attempting to understand what it would mean to heed this plea.

As the preceding summary shows, the *Republic* is not a systematic treatise that lays down a complete, polished argument but an evolving, frequently interrupted discussion that contains many digressions and ends in paradox. Most important, the liberation of the young men's *erōs* within the context of the unfolding discussion and the emphasis on recollection on the narrative level of the *Republic* contrasts sharply with the restriction of *erōs* and the institutionalization of forgetfulness and deception within the City of Adeimantus and the Kallipolis. Finally, the fact that Socrates' young friends repeatedly challenge him, and that the discussion again and again seems to be finished but turns out not to be, should make us wary of accepting anything Socrates says as the final word on the subject. We too must constantly challenge Socrates, for his argument, it appears, is by no means complete.[8]

MYTH: PHILOSOPHY AS EPIC QUEST

Philosophical Ascent and Descent   The *Republic*'s narrative, argumentative, and dramatic structures become fully visible and intelligible only when seen in relation to its mythical structure. Once again, the connection between these structural dimensions is introduced at the beginning of the *Republic*. The dialogue's first word is *katebēn* ("I went down"). The Piraeus is down country from Athens, but Socrates' descent to the Piraeus must be understood metaphorically as well as literally. A number of clues suggest that Socrates' journey to the Piraeus is to be understood as a metaphorical descent into the underworld:

(a) The poets traditionally situate Hades, the land of the dead, beyond a body of water. Homer and Hesiod speak of Hades as bounded by Ocean and the river Styx; in Socrates' Myth of Er the land of the dead lies across the river of Carelessness in the plain of Forgetfulness. Piraeus, in turn, means "Beyond-Land"—specifically, the land beyond the river thought to have once separated the region of the Piraeus from the rest of Attica.[9]

(b) Bendis is a deity of the underworld, and the torch-race and all-night vigil in her honor, which take place in the Piraeus concurrently with the dialogue, "are enactments of the continuing life of the sun's light and of the promise of the sun's renewal after its descent into the realm of perpetual night" (Rosenstock, 220-21).

(c) The *Republic*'s characters and dramatic setting give the dialogue a strong undertone of death and violence. The conversation with which the *Republic* begins centers on the figure of Cephalus, whom Socrates calls "very old" and speaks of as being on "the threshold of old age," meaning the threshold of death (328c-e). One ancient source indicates that Cephalus actually died at least 20 years before the dramatic date of the *Republic*. Furthermore, deadly violence ultimately engulfs those present. In 404 B.C. the Peloponnesian War is lost and the Thirty Tyrants tyrannize over the Athenians and execute Polemarchus and Niceratus. The following year, Lysias helps to overthrow the Thirty in a vicious battle fought in the Piraeus and swirling around the Temple of Bendis. One of the repercussions of this episode of tyranny is the conviction and execution of Socrates, whom the Athenians resent partly because Critias, the leader of the Thirty, is known to have associated with him.[10]

(d) Descent into and ascent from the underworld is a recurring theme in the myths told in the *Republic*. In book 2 Glaucon tells the tale of a man who went down into a chasm that opened in the earth in order to strip the ring off of a giant corpse (359c-60b). In book 3 Socrates explains that the rulers of the city-in-speech will tell the citizens a Noble Lie—namely, that they were all reared beneath the surface of the earth (414d-15c). In book 7 Socrates compares human experience to the situation of prisoners within a cave and compares the cave itself, from which the philosopher alone is capable of ascending, to Hades (514a-517a). Finally, book 10 concludes with the Myth of Er, a man who went down as an observer into a place Socrates identifies with Hades (619a), remembered what he saw there, and ascended to the land of the living to make his report (614b-21b). Er's journey mythically reiterates Socrates' descent to the Piraeus to see the sights, his return to Athens, and his recollection of the previous night's events. The Myth of Er ends when Er awakens at dawn on his funeral pyre, and we may well imagine that it is around dawn when Socrates finishes narrating Er's tale. The simultaneous conclusions at dawn of the dialogue, the Festival of Bendis, and the Myth of Er reinforce the suggestion that the conversation of the *Republic* takes place, metaphorically, in Hades.

If we may judge by its setting, the *Republic*, like Homer's epic poems, is an extended confrontation with death (cf. Segal 1978, 322-23). Two further observations are necessary at this point. First, there is a promise of rebirth and renewal at the conclusion of the *Republic*. Socrates' narration of Er's ascent from Hades is paralleled by the simultaneous emergence of the sun at dawn after its journey through the underworld—a journey ritually reenacted in the torch-race and all-night vigil of the Bendis festival. Second, the *Republic* does not represent the philosophic quest as a unidirectional process. To begin with, Socrates' initial, metaphoric descent makes possible the erotic, philosophic ascent of his young companions over the course of the dialogue. The intertwined themes of descent and ascent, which are explicitly present in the *Republic*'s myths, also structure the movement of the philosophic drama as a whole. At the end of book 4 Socrates says to Glaucon that they have reached a "lookout point" in the logos or argument (445c). At the beginning of book 5, however, Socrates represents himself and his friends as trying to make their way up a slippery and dangerous path, as if attempting to climb out of a cave (450e-51a). The logos continues to "ascend" until it reaches the topics of the Good and the education of the philosopher in books 6 and 7 and then "descends" once again, in books 8 and 9, into the cavelike realm of political community. In book 10 the dialogue's double, shuttling movement is mythically reflected in the two paths Er sees in the underworld: one leading upward into heaven for souls that have lived justly, and the other leading down into the earth for unjust souls (614c). Finally, Socrates' initial descent to the Piraeus is balanced by his ascent and return to Athens after the conclusion of the dialogue but prior to its narration.

Like the action of book 1, the images of the Sun, Line, and Cave confirm that our prephilosophic experience points "upward" toward philosophy. The initial appearance of focal topics and themes on a "low," relatively unreflective level of discourse anticipates their subsequent treatment on a "higher," more comprehensive, but also more abstract level, while the adequacy of this "higher" understanding is, in turn, tested by its power to illuminate that which we first encounter on the "lower" level of ordinary or prephilosophic experience. In addition, we find anticipation and repetition on the dialogue's "horizontal" axis as well: the levels of experience first encountered during the ascent that takes place in the first half of the *Republic* will be traversed once again in the phase of descent and recapitulation in its second half. In this respect, the *Republic* resembles early Greek poetry (e.g., the *Iliad*) in that it is "composed on the plan of concentric rings: the themes on the diameter reappear in reverse order as if they were reflected through a central axis" (Brann, 7).

The latter observations begin to explain the doubling-back of the logos noted earlier, and perhaps also Socrates' decision to remain in the Piraeus. The higher and the lower cannot be severed, for they are interdependent: philosophy measures, and at the same time measures itself by, prephilosophical experience. The Festival of Bendis fittingly reinforces the philosophic interconnection of the higher and the lower: the circular journey of the sun as it moves above and below the earth's surface seems to be a cosmic analogue of the movement of philosophy itself.

Philosophy and Mystery Initiation   The Festival of Bendis is important in another respect as well: the dramatic and mythical dimensions of the *Republic* on one level imitate the structure of initiation into the Mysteries, particularly those that took place at Eleusis, with which most Athenians were probably familiar. In the Eleusinian Mysteries initiates participated in certain secret rites associated with Demeter and her daughter Kore (or Persephone), deities of the earth and the underworld. Bendis, we recall, is a goddess of the underworld. In addition, the structure of the Mysteries reflected the theme of descent into and return from Hades. The rites at Eleusis reenacted the mythical abduction of Kore by Hades, god of the underworld, and Demeter's search for and discovery of her daughter. Like the adventures of Er and the conversation of the *Republic*, the Mysteries required an initiate to make a passage or journey through the night that is initially disorienting, to engage in new and strange deeds and listen to new and strange speeches, and to behold fearsome and fantastic sights (compare the description of the tyrant's soul at 588c-89a with 615d-16a); the journey is concluded at dawn, with a return to light. Initiation thus involved the ritual death and rebirth of the initiate. Membership in the community of the initiated was conceived as a special source of well-being.[11]

Given the structural parallels just noted, we may expect that the drama of the *Republic* centers on the beginning of philosophy, or the initiation into philosophy of the previously uninitiated.[12] We shall also find that the *Republic* attempts to answer the implications of Aristophanes' portrayal of Socratic teaching as a perversion of the Mysteries (*Clouds*, 140-43, 254*ff*). Whereas the *Clouds* suggests that Socratic philosophizing undermines our sense of the sacred and corrupts the bonds of human community, the subtext of religious initiation in the *Republic* implies that the pursuit of philosophic wisdom may bind human beings together into a community of friendship that is in its own way both sacred and concerned with things divine.

The *Republic* suggests that the philosopher requires a sense of the proper "place" of his own philosophic activity. We may now develop this insight by considering the metaphor of Hades in the *Republic*, as well as the themes of mythical and philosophical descent and ascent, within the context of the ancient poetic tradition.

The *Republic* and the *Odyssey*   The motif of a quest to the underworld was already well-established in Mediterranean legend by the time of Plato. Various versions of such a quest are depicted in *Gilgamesh*, an epic poem composed prior to 2000 B.C. that has aptly been called "the *Odyssey* of the Babylonians."[13] Similar quests are reflected in the Greek legends of Orpheus, Heracles, and Odysseus, all of whom the poets represent as having at some point journeyed to Hades; Aristophanes' comic version of the same theme is to be found in the adventures of Dionysus in the *Frogs*.

For the reader of the *Republic*, the most important of these stories is Homer's tale of Odysseus. Like *Gilgamesh*, the *Odyssey* is an epic of return, in which the hero must pass beyond the boundary of death to achieve the wisdom that allows him to return, renewed and, as it were, reborn, to life. The process of return in the *Odyssey* falls into three successive stages: Odysseus's adventures in the fantastic realm of monsters, goddesses, and dead souls, during which he loses all of his companions; his sojourn among the peaceful Phaeacians, whose nearness to the gods and freedom from cares, pain, and toil betoken their distance from things human; and his return to the real, violent world of Ithaca. The wandering Odysseus repeatedly encounters death in each stage of his return and in many different guises, as is clear from the imagery that Homer borrows from more ancient poetry and develops over the course of the *Odyssey*. Death comes to be linked with darkness, sleep, and forgetfulness, and is topographically associated with caves: Odysseus's path leads not only to the cavernous region of Hades but also to the dark, cavelike harbor of the cannibalistic Laestrygonians and the island caves of the Cyclops and

Calypso. Life, correspondingly, is associated with light, wakefulness, and recollection.[14]

For Odysseus, life is ultimately inseparable from hearth, home, and the community of his fellow Greeks: to live means not merely to exist but to return home. In order "to win his own life [*psuchē*; literally, "soul"] and the return of his comrades,"[15] Odysseus is compelled to cross the sea to the underworld, so that the shade of the prophet Teiresias may instruct him in his journey. Odysseus returns from Hades equipped not only with the knowledge of how to get home, but also with deeper insight into the nature of life and death. The vision of phantom existence he is vouchsafed in the underworld helps him to continue to steer clear of the various forms of living death that present themselves over the course of his journey, just as he has already resisted the honeyed, memory-laundering drugs of Circe and the Lotus Eaters—potions that make men lose all desire and thought for their homelands (*Odyssey*, 9.82*ff*, 10.274*ff*). For Odysseus, as for Gilgamesh, homecoming means something both less and more than the literal avoidance of death: even after witnessing the gloomy sights of Hades, Odysseus guarantees his own death by refusing the lovely goddess Calypso's offer to grant him immortality if he will remain with her (*Odyssey*, 5.136). Although Odysseus thereby effectively chooses physical death, there is a sense in which he wins his life or soul by rejecting a life that is not worth living—an eternity of anonymous isolation on Calypso's depressing island, where he "is like the shades of the underworld in his listlessness and sorrow" (Frame, 74).

Like the *Odyssey*, the *Republic* is an extended journey in which the movement of the logos metaphorically involves sailing (394d), descents into dark, slippery, cavelike regions, most strikingly in connection with the City of Adeimantus (427c-d, 432c, 450e-51a), and being shipwrecked and forced to swim through the sea (441c, 453d). Most important, allusions to Odysseus's journey into and return from the underworld frame the action of the *Republic*. Socrates' first words echo the beginning of Odysseus's narration of his descent into Hades for his wife, Penelope: "*katebēn domon Aidos eisō*" ("I went down into the house of Hades" [*Odyssey*, 23.252]). Socrates' last words in the dialogue mention Odysseus by name. The Myth of Er, Socrates puns, is not a "tale of Alkinoos [*Alkinou*]," Odysseus's royal Phaeacian host, but of Er, "a strong [*alkimou*] man" (614b). In Hades Er sees souls choosing their future lives, and frequently making terrible mistakes in the process. But he observes one soul that stands out because it recollects and takes to heart the lessons of its former life and consequently chooses a good future life (620c-d). That soul, whose careful choice underscores the power of philosophic recollection, is the soul of Odysseus. Finally, in relating the image of the Cave, Socrates quotes from that part of the *Odyssey* in which Odysseus, having descended into the underworld, is told by the shade of Achilles that he would rather be a serf to a poor man on earth than ruler over all the dead (516d). The effect of this quotation is to link the situation of human beings in a political community with that of the shades in Hades, and the situation of the philosopher, whose quest for wisdom enables him to transcend the cavelike horizons of a political community, with that of Odysseus, a visitor to Hades.

In connecting the philosopher and the fate of the logos concerning the city-in-speech with Odysseus and his adventures, Plato suggests that in the *Republic* Socrates narrates a new, specifically *philosophic* odyssey. This observation provides us with a fruitful way of understanding both the nature of philosophy and the plot or plan of the *Republic*. Prior to philosophizing, Plato implies, the soul, like Odysseus, is somehow in exile, a wanderer in a kind of no-man's-land suspended between life and death. Philosophy, in turn, attempts a kind of "homecoming" for human beings—not a literal, physical homecoming but a metaphysical homecoming of the soul. The *Republic*'s Homeric subtext encourages us to envision philosophy as a quest whose goal is the return of the soul to its original and proper place within the cosmos or Whole. As in the *Odyssey*, death, darkness, forgetfulness, and placelessness are joined in this vision, as are life, light, recollection, and homecoming: as Socrates' images of the Sun and the Cave suggest, the homeward quest of the displaced soul is also a return to light and life from ways of living death.

The *Republic*, however, calls into question the presuppositions of the philosophic quest in a way that underscores its deeply problematic nature. There is in particular an important difference between the philosophic odyssey and that of Odysseus himself: Odysseus is sure of his goal in a way that the philosopher is not. Odysseus knows well the home he longs for; it is, after all, his birthplace and his kingdom. He knows what home is and where it is, and he knows its name: Ithaca. In this respect, the difference between the *Odyssey* and the *Republic* is significant: whereas Odysseus is never more than a visitor in the island caverns of Polyphemus and Calypso, human beings, including the philosopher, are born into (and most never leave) the subterranean phantom world of the cave. How, then, can the philosopher be sure, prior to the completion of his quest, that there is any such home place, or any such Whole, as he envisions? Without some assurance about these things, what reasons does the philosopher have for believing that philosophy is either meaningful or possible?

Since only a fool or a madman would devote his life to an impossible and meaningless quest, the philosopher must be centrally concerned with understanding and justifying his own philosophic activity. The *Republic* will necessarily reflect the centrality of these concerns as well. But since the reflexive attempt to establish its own legitimacy is a crucial part of the philosophic quest, a problem arises concerning how this quest gets under way in the first place.

The problem of the beginning of philosophy comes to light when one reflects on the difference between the painful homesickness that motivates Odysseus and the soul's initial metaphysical contentment. Philosophy may at first seem entirely unnecessary: we may feel perfectly at home in the familiar contexts within which we have been born and raised. These prephilosophic contexts have, after all, shaped our desires and beliefs, have impressed on us judgments of the goals and paths of life, and thereby have helped to mold who we are. Philosophy, however, presupposes the disconcerting realization that the conventional habitats furnished by *nomos*—the shared opinions, customs, and traditions of our political communities—are at bottom unfamiliar and foreign to us. How do we come to experience this realization?

While Plato addresses the latter questions, he also indicates that we need philosophy even if we never recognize this need. The philosophic quest represented in the *Republic* therefore involves, in the phases both of ascent and descent, several encounters with disorient-ed and fragmented souls. The first such encounter is that of Socrates with Cephalus, whose life, like that of the Cyclops Polyphemus, revolves narrowly around the needs and desires of his body. The model provided by the *Odyssey* helps to explain why these con-frontations are necessary. Just as Odysseus must overcome the chal-lenges of monsters, the blandishments of various forms of living death, and the terrors of a visit to Hades, one cannot recognize one's need for a philosophic education, let alone begin to acquire such an education, without critically exploring the alternately threatening and seductive panoply of unexamined lives and attempting to over-come the antiphilosophic challenges they represent. We are again reminded of the shuttling movement of the logos: one cannot ascend philosophically without descending by inquiry into the depths of human souls.

Plato seems to have had at least three general reasons for using the *Odyssey* as the *Republic*'s primary mythical subtext. First, the philosophic appropriation of Homer dramatically suits Plato's inten-tion to challenge the Greek poeticoreligious tradition that Homer largely founded. Second, the *Odyssey* lends itself to such appropria-tion, because it is in important respects a profoundly philosophical work. Homer's epic poem may be interpreted as a voyage of deepen-ing self-knowledge, in which the hero's homeward journey involves a growing understanding of the whole of human experience and the rejection of ways of life that fail to recognize, and recollectively to internalize, essential elements of that experience. The philosophic sug-gestiveness of this interpretation is strengthened by evidence that *noos* or *nous*, the "mind" or "intelligence" that distinguishes Odysseus from his forgetful comrades, and *nostos*, the "homecoming" that intelli-gence enables and by which it is in turn tested and strengthened, are derived from a common Indo-European root **nes-*, meaning some-thing like "return to light and life" (Frame; see esp. 34-80 on the essential role played by *nous* in Odysseus's return). This original con-nection between *nous* and *nostos* informs Plato's presentation of phi-losophy in the *Republic* as well. According to Socrates, it is the capacity of *nous* that allows us to see the Ideas in the light of the Good and so to complete our emergence from the cave and find our way about in the light of the sun (508d).

A third reason for Plato's use of the *Odyssey* as a mythical subtext is that Homer's episodic representation of the voyage of the soul fits Plato's specific philosophic purposes. Odysseus's homecoming represents on one level his gradual discovery of the real and essential character of human experience. This process of discovery requires Odysseus to move through realms of illusion or fantasy on his way to reality (Segal 1962, 17*ff*). Plato makes philosophic use not only of this general distinction between fantasy and reality, or what merely appears to be and what genuinely is, but also of the particular stages of Odysseus's return to reality as well. Perhaps most important, the logos itself, in passing through the three great waves of paradox in book 5 that must be endured in order to move from the City of Adeimantus to the Kallipolis (457b-d, 472a), makes a transition analogous to that undergone by Odysseus when, in book 5 of the *Odyssey*, he leaves Calypso's island cave and the "unreal, dreamlike world of monsters and enchantresses" (Segal 1962, 17) and takes to the sea (cf. Brann, 22; Segal 1978, 329; Planinc, 277-79). Three great waves push Odysseus into a detour whereby he arrives at Scheria, the more recognizably human but nevertheless isolated, sheltered, and consequently still rather "unreal" island of the Phaeacians, who in their pleasant and carefree existence are "near of kin to the gods" (*Odyssey*, 5.35). Socrates' elaboration of the Kallipolis in books 5 through 7, we recall, constitutes an expository detour into which he is forced by his companions.

The aforementioned Homeric parallel underscores the deficiencies of both the City of Adeimantus and Glaucon's Kallipolis. Odysseus falls into a profound depression while he is with Calypso: he spends his days "look[ing] over the unresting sea, shedding tears" (*Odyssey*, 5.84). Odysseus's depression arises from his experience of a kind of living death: Calypso's name underscores the sense in which she "covers over" or "buries" (*kaluptei*) his life by detaining him at her cave (cf. Dimock, 412: "Kalypso is oblivion"). Similarly, Socrates implies that Adeimantus's dark, cavelike city, in which humans are trained like animals and even the rulers lack philosophy, is itself a fantastic domain of living death that frustrates the deepest human longings. Yet the Kallipolis, which includes wisdom but does still greater violence to human nature than Adeimantus's regime, is no less defective because of its "remoteness" from human life. The Odyssean subtext is quite suggestive in this connection: the Phaeacian rulers Alkinoos and Arete— King "Mighty-Mind" and Queen "Virtue"—provide a Homeric analog to the humanly impossible hegemony of intellect and virtue in the Kallipolis. Socrates' account of the Kallipolis is thus *itself* the "tale of Alkinoos" that is somehow superseded by the Myth of Er (614b).

Just as Odysseus feels compelled to leave Scheria, the defects of the Kallipolis can be remedied only by exploring the sources and implications of its remoteness and in this sense "returning" to human life. The higher, once separated from the lower, must be rewoven with it. For this reason, the *Republic* does not end with the Kallipolis: the descent from the Kallipolis in the second half of the dialogue, together with Socrates' shift in focus from the nature of the best regime to the problem of individual salvation, accomplishes precisely such a return to human reality from the "dream" of the just city (443b). While Socrates alludes to the beginning of Homer's *Iliad* in introducing his account of the internecine conflict by which the Kallipolis decays (545d), the tour of regimes and corresponding human characters he undertakes in books 8 and 9 is even more reminiscent of Odysseus, who "saw the towns and learned the mind [*noon*] of many human beings"—or, on an alternative reading, "learned the *nomos* of many human beings" (*Odyssey*, 1.3; cf. Socrates' allusion to the Lotus Eaters at 560c). Socrates' tour of regimes and souls makes it clear that the community cannot be saved along with the individual, as he had initially hoped (497a). Similarly, one should recall that the homecoming of Odysseus was accomplished at heavy cost to the Phaeacians as a whole, since it resulted in their permanent isolation from the rest of the mortal world (*Odyssey*, 13.125*ff*). The mythical correlate of the dialogue's return to reality is thus the sleeping Odysseus's nighttime voyage from Scheria to Ithaca, which, like the *Republic* itself, concludes at dawn (*Odyssey*, 13.93-95).[16]

I have stressed the role of the *Odyssey* within the mythical structure of the *Republic*, yet Plato's work contains many allusions and more than one mythical subtext. Eva Brann, for example (in Brann, 9-12), observes that the *Republic* concerns the essentially Heraclean theme of the relation of virtue to happiness and argues that over the course of the dialogue Socrates reenacts Heracles' descent into Hades to bring up the monster Cerberus (the mythical equivalent of the tyrant's soul, which Socrates finally succeeds in bringing to light in book 9). With regard to the motif of heroic descent, the Heraclean and Odyssean subtexts complement one another, yet in other respects Plato's allusions to Odysseus are philosophically more provocative. Most important, the comparison of the philosopher with Odysseus rather sharply poses the problem of the distinction between philosophy and sophistry. Heracles represents tremendous power and endurance in the service of virtue; Odysseus is physically less overwhelming but so much more complex in mind and character as to be fundamentally questionable.[17]

In the first line of the *Odyssey* Homer calls Odysseus *polutropos*, meaning both a "much-wandering" man and a man "of many turns or wiles." After Homer, Odysseus's clever deceitfulness threatens to overshadow his *nous*: whereas in Sophocles' *Ajax* and Euripides' *Cyclops* Odysseus's shifting and shifty character arguably represents postheroic political virtue, in Euripides' *Hecuba* and Sophocles' *Philoctetes* he is less ambiguously depicted as a self-serving sophist. Socratic questioning resembles sophistry in that it has the effect of undermining one's prephilosophic trust in *nomos*, and thus of loosening the bonds that tie one to one's own political community. And as we shall see, the *Republic* shows that, in argument, the Socratic philosopher—like Odysseus and the sophists—is polytropic. Socrates' resemblance to the paradoxical and provocative figure of Odysseus emphasizes the seriousness of the charges against Socrates first formulated by Aristophanes.

PHILOSOPHY AND POLITICS

The *Republic* immediately takes up the challenge of responding to Aristophanes' question about the extent to which community—

philosophical or political—is possible at all. Genuine community presupposes logos—reasonable speech that is capable of articulating shared standards of worth, as opposed to merely instrumental speech in the service of personal, private desires. The possibility of community therefore depends on the relationship between speech and desire. In this connection, it is crucial to observe that the Athenians' commitment to traditional conceptions of virtue had eroded markedly by the late fifth century. Let us call this political atmosphere "post-traditional." When *erōs* shrinks to become a love exclusively of one's own things, it is self-enclosed in a way that entails injustice and undercuts logos; both political community and Socratic philosophizing, however, presuppose a degree—although surely not the same degree—of erotic openness. Perhaps it is not too misleading to say that in the post-traditional situation, the health of the polis seems to depend on the possibility of philosophic education: *both* philosophy and political community require that *erōs* be opened up and turned toward the quest for shared knowledge of the just, the good, and the noble.

This is by no means to say that philosophic and political education are identical, or even that philosophy and political community are ultimately compatible. The fundamental issue to which Aristophanes calls our attention—that of the politically problematic nature of philosophic wonder—is underscored and extended by the *Republic*'s prologue, the conflicting treatment of *erōs* in its argumentative and dramatic dimensions, and its mythical structure and Odyssean subtext. Our reflections on this mythical subtext suggest a number of interconnected questions about the relationship between philosophy and politics. In what ways is prephilosophic life disoriented and fragmented, and how is this disorientation dependent on the displacement or placelessness of our conventional habitats? How does philosophy initiate and enable the homeward turning and return of the soul? Is the quest for wisdom meaningful independently of the achievement of its goal? If not, is there ultimately any significant difference between philosophy and sophistry?[18]

Let us begin to explore these questions in the home of Polemarchus.

6

A Host of Challenges

In book 1 Socrates' philosophic way of life is challenged by Cephalus, Polemarchus, Cleitophon, and Thrasymachus. The antagonistic drama played out in these pages displays both the qualities of soul that enable philosophic education and the antiphilosophic traits that impede it. Socrates' encounters with Cephalus and Cleitophon mark the limits of philosophy's power to interest or engage human beings. If Socrates, like Odysseus, seeks "to win his soul and the return of his comrades," then Cephalus and Cleitophon are beyond salvation. But Socrates is able to meet the attacks of Polemarchus and Thrasymachus, whose names emphasize their spiritedness (Thrasymachus means "Bold in Battle"), in such a way as to draw these men into a common philosophic inquiry. In fact, the motif of battle helps to explain how Socrates is able to turn the conversation toward philosophy. Spiritedness (*thumos*) is the tough fiber of a striving, fighting soul; it is the word for a warrior's "heart" in Homer's *Iliad*. As we shall see, the action of book 1 begins to establish that the potential philosopher must be highly spirited as well as highly erotic.

Socrates' main interlocutors are nevertheless very different: whereas Polemarchus is a solid patriot, Thrasymachus is a politically cynical intellectual. Insofar as these two men are open to philosophic reflection, they are so in different ways and for different reasons. Each one, in turn, is paired with a similar yet educationally closed soul: Polemarchus with Cephalus and Thrasymachus with Cleitophon. Furthermore, Polemarchus and Thrasymachus respectively anticipate, in their natures and their arguments, Adeimantus and Glaucon—the relatively superior interlocutors who come to dominate the remainder of the Republic. The participants in the dialogue represent successively better images of the characteristics of the philosophically inclined soul. In this way Plato teaches his readers in deed no less than in speech. Let us turn now to the details of this exemplary lesson.

CEPHALUS: THE SOUL AS CLOSED CIRCLE

When Socrates and his companions enter Polemarchus's house, they take seats in a circle around Cephalus, who, as the venerable paterfamilias, occupies the position of honor at the center of this gathering. Socrates makes Cephalus the focus of the ensuing discussion as well. The name Cephalus is a Platonic pun. The old man is physically little more than a head (*kephalē*): his corporeal strength, desires, and pleasures have by now withered away in him (328c-d). In addition, Cephalus is the head of Polemarchus's family. As such, he sets an example for his sons, and his speeches and deeds command the respect paternal authority claims as its due. Cephalus's familial authority, in turn, supports and is supported by the traditional authority of civic religion. Cephalus wears on his head the wreath he wore while making sacrifices at Polemarchus's courtyard altar, presumably to *Zeus herkeios*, "Zeus, protector of the household" (Adam, 328*cn*). The conversation with Cephalus takes place within the sanctified, private space of the family.

As always in Plato, setting anticipates content. Tradition, together with the power nature grants fathers over their children, has placed Cephalus in the role of a guide and model for his sons. Socrates is most interested in exploring Cephalus's legitimacy in this role and, by extension, the legitimacy of the civic tradition in which his understanding of piety is rooted. Apart from outward manifestations of deference and politeness, to what extent does Cephalus deserve to be emulated in speech and deed? To what extent do the customs and conventional beliefs by which Cephalus takes his bearings provide appropriate guidance for the soul? Socrates begins to raise these questions immediately. At stake are the related issues of Cephalus's character, the adequacy of Athenian *nomos*, and the best way of life. In the background of this discussion stands the *Clouds*: in pursuing the latter issues, Socrates runs the usual risk of usurping a father's prerogatives and seeming to corrupt his sons. He presses Cephalus as one would a traveler who has explored a road "that *perhaps* we too will have to take" (328e; my italics). Like Er, Cephalus, who is "on the threshold" of death (328e), will relate what he has seen on his journey. The problem of choice that is raised in the Myth of Er is implicit in the present context as well. In particular, Socrates' wording suggests that we may not be *compelled* to follow Cephalus's particular path of life; whether anyone would *choose* to do so depends on how well one understands the old man's report.

Cephalus begins by noting that when he gets together to talk with his old friends, most of them recollect the pleasures of sex, drink, and feasts they can no longer enjoy. This is an occasion for despair: like the shades in Hades, these old men think that they "had then lived well, but are now not even alive." Cephalus, however, is of a different opinion. Old age in fact brings "great peace and freedom," for when the bodily desires slacken one is freed from "very many mad masters." Cephalus concludes his description of the view from old age by implying that he has borne both youth and old age well because he is "balanced [*kosmios*] and good-tempered." Cephalus thus suggests that his soul, like the cosmos, is a well-ordered whole (328e-29d).

Cephalus's speech fills Socrates with wonder (329d), most likely because of the striking disparity between the bulk of the speech and its concluding praise of good character. Cephalus indicates that before the body weakens it rules the soul, in that all men live for the satisfaction of bodily desires. His description of corporeal compulsion is most vivid: insofar as the passions hold dominion as "frenzied," "savage," and "mad" masters (329c-d), reason is their slave. Freedom is negatively defined as the release, in old age, from bondage to corporeal *erōs*. Yet quite apart from physical infirmity is a sense in which most old men are still slaves to their bodies: they wistfully focus their capacities of speech and recollection, two essential powers of their souls, on the past pleasures of their bodies.

Cephalus's speech offers us a model of desire, conversation, and recollection that conflicts in every respect with the Socratic paradigm. Cephalus's *erōs* begins and ends with sexual lust. Despite his suggestion to the contrary (328d), noncorporeal *erōs*, and specifically the desire for philosophic discourse, does not blossom in the twilight years of man: he leaves as soon as the conversation takes a philosophic turn. Furthermore, given the general picture Cephalus paints of the human condition, his suggestion that good character has helped him to bear life well betrays a profound lack of self-reflection. In youth Cephalus's soul was far from well-ordered, for he was a slave to raging passions. If his old age is less tempestuous, is it not only because of the passage of time?

Cephalus is nonetheless eager to emphasize his moderation: he stands as a mean between his grandfather's money-making zeal and his father's free spending. Socrates has an explanation for the different dispositions of Cephalus's grandfather and father toward money: while those who do not make their own money are serious only about spending it, moneymakers feel an additional attachment to their wealth because it is the product of their own work. Socrates implies that men are especially attached to that which is their own and that which is useful to them. Cephalus must feel this double attachment to the money he has made. In fact, his fondness for wealth is bound up with his fondness for his children: he states that he hopes to leave his sons more than he himself inherited (330a-c).

The love of one's own things, Socrates implies, is natural to human beings. It is also an ambiguous sentiment of great political and philosophical importance. It holds the family and the polis together but by the same token may exclude that which lies outside of a narrow circle of self-interest, including the welfare of the political community as a whole. The love of one's own things also blinds one to one's own defects and is hence an obstacle to the critical reflection that enables philosophic ascent: moneymakers, Socrates says, are willing to praise nothing but money; poets are similarly attached to their poems, fathers to their children, and, we may add, men to their own bodies and opinions and cities to their own traditions (330c). Whether philosophical and political virtue can coexist thus seems to depend on whether these attachments can be opened up to education without being destroyed.

Cephalus loves his own things in an exclusive, narrow, and inflexible manner. Despite his self-centeredness, however, he appears to look beyond himself in one respect: he sacrifices to the gods. What Cephalus reveals about the origins of his religious attitude helps us to understand men like himself, and it thereby sheds light on the limitations of traditional piety.

Cephalus introduces the topic of the gods in response to Socrates' next question: What is the greatest good Cephalus has enjoyed from possessing great wealth? Cephalus starts by noting that not many would be persuaded by what he has to say, evidently because the persuasiveness of his speech depends on the experience of being on the threshold of death. He explains that the tales told by the poets about Hades—tales that seem laughable to the young—make men who are close to death fear that they will be punished in the afterlife for their unjust deeds and cause them for the first time to think about the conduct of their lives. The "suspicion" and "terror" to which this fear gives rise makes one "reckon up his accounts" and often even wake from sleep in a fright (330d-e).

For Cephalus, the path to self-knowledge begins only with the fear of death and is rooted in self-love. Before facing death, he suggests, men are asleep in that they give no serious thought to living justly, let alone to the question of the best life. (Yet Socrates and his young friends will stay awake all night examining just these issues.) The reason for their thoughtlessness and their subsequent fears is evident from what Cephalus has already told us: before their bodies decay, men are willing slaves to corporeal *erōs*, and the "mad masters" that drive them toward bodily pleasures inevitably lead them to commit injustice. Injustice arises from *erōs* and so is more familiar to men than justice— which is perhaps why injustice is mentioned before justice in the

Republic, the first mention of either being in the present passage. Insofar as it helps one to keep from committing injustice, however, money is useful in living a just and pious life and thus maintaining sweet hopes for the afterlife such as Pindar describes. Cephalus maintains that, for the decent man in particular, money "contributes a great deal to not cheating or lying to any man against one's will, and, moreover, to not departing for that other place frightened because one owes some sacrifices to a god or money to a human being." Money is especially useful in this way, he concludes, to a man who possesses intelligence (*nous*; 330d-31b).

Cephalus's response to Socrates' question about wealth completes his picture of the human condition. Once again, his speech emphasizes the soul's moral and intellectual enslavement to the body and thereby explodes his pretensions to self-knowledge. Cephalus prides himself on being decent and intelligent, yet his speech explains decency in terms of fear and money and emphasizes the purely calculative or instrumental nature of *nous*. In youth, men are mastered by mad desires; Cephalus now adds that, before they are frightened by the approach of death, men neither think nor care about justice; indeed, they laugh at the prospect of punishment. Fear activates self-interested calculation and is evidently the root of whatever decency we may possess, for fear alone makes us think about doing justice to the gods as well as to men. In addition, Cephalus makes it clear that without money even a "good" man like himself would be compelled to lie and cheat against his will. Finally, money is essential to piety as well as justice. The pious man does justice to the gods by paying them what they are owed—namely, sacrifices.

Cephalus's thoroughly conventional piety is deeply flawed: he has no sense of the sacred. For him, worship, like justice, is purely instrumental. Cephalus sacrifices to the gods not out of reverent awe before that which is inviolably holy but out of fear for himself. Because his relations with men and gods are entirely self-serving, he is inclined to understand all such relations in terms of monetary transactions. In particular, Socrates' encounter with Cephalus points toward the potential perversion of the practice of sacrifice into an essentially commercial activity (cf. *Euthyphro*, 14d-e). Cephalus acts as if the gods run a protection racket; because they are stronger than humans, they must be paid off with sacrifices. It does not occur to him that the gods may take umbrage at bribes (cf. Plato, *Alcibiades II*, 149e). Cephalus never looks beyond the narrow circle of his own things after all, even in worship.

Cephalus also raises the issue of the rivalry between philosophy and poetry. In his view, the wisdom of the poets is unsurpassed. Besides citing Sophocles as an authority regarding erotic madness (329b-c), Cephalus makes it clear that the poets' tales are crucial to his religious orientation. In particular, he is moved by their alternately fearful and hopeful depictions of the afterlife. Because they tell stories about the gods that both stir up and attempt to calm deep-seated fears, the poets are partly responsible for Cephalus's defective conception of piety. The visceral fear Cephalus describes turns one inward toward oneself, not outward toward the sacred. True piety seems to require courage, insofar as openness to that which is above and beyond oneself is at odds with fearful self-obsession. One needs courage also in order to obtain knowledge of the divine things, because fear tends to breed superstition, while the hopeful stories we tell ourselves to allay our fears are often just wishful thinking.

The Cephalus section begins to undercut the validity of the poets' religious myths, and, by extension, the claim of the poets to wisdom. While the poets' tales about the afterlife play upon great fears and hopes, both knowledge of things divine and openness to the sacred require a detachment from selfish fears and hopes. Socrates, we may note, displays precisely this kind of detachment, both in living and in dying. Perhaps the courage that allows Socrates to step beyond fearful self-obsession may also serve as the basis for a philosophic piety that genuinely acknowledges the sacred.

"What you say is very fine indeed, Cephalus" (331b). Socrates' words are clearly laden with irony: Cephalus's account of himself is singularly ugly and base, not least because of its self-delusive quality. Socrates' ironic praise is perhaps an instance of the principle he goes on to set forth—namely, that it is unjust to return weapons or tell the whole truth to a mad friend (331c). Cephalus is not literally mad; indeed, he is sober and calculating in his old age, although in his youth he was enslaved to the "mad masters" of erotic passion. But whereas *sōphronein*, "being of sound mind," implies possessing both *sōphrosunē* ("self-control" or "moderation") and *phronēsis* ("intelligent judgment," especially about one's own life), Cephalus is immoderately concerned with the things of the body and lacks self-knowledge.

Socrates' discussion with Cephalus takes place, metaphorically, in the depths of the cave, a region to which we return at the end of the *Republic*. In his skin-deep virtue and tyrannical appetites, Cephalus anticipates in particular the soul Er observes choosing the greatest tyranny (619b-c). Like that soul, Cephalus is utterly unreflective and unwilling to accept responsibility for his own actions: he walks away from the conversation when the possibility of self-criticism is raised (331c-d). In name as well as nature, Cephalus points toward the enchained heads (*tas kephalas*, 514b) of the lowest cave-dwellers. Imprisoned as he is within the circle of habitual self-obsession, he is beyond the reach of philosophy.

POLEMARCHUS AND FRIENDSHIP:
OPENING THE CIRCLE

Like an ancient beacon, Cephalus marks a well-worn path of life—a singularly un-self-conscious and ignoble path, the *Republic* suggests, of which fellow travelers would do well to steer clear. Socrates now faces an immediate challenge with regard to Polemarchus, for in going off to sacrifice Cephalus passes the torch to his oldest son, the heir to his argument as well as his property (331d-e; cf. Plato, *Laws*, 776b, in which the continuity of successive generations is compared to a torch-race). When Cephalus leaves, Socrates attempts to occupy with philosophy the paternal space he vacates. Polemarchus had said earlier that he and his companions would not listen to Socrates, and even joked about using force against him (327c). Socrates, it seems, must convince Polemarchus that philosophy, like his own aged father, deserves a respectful hearing. In order to do so, he proceeds to draw out perplexities in Polemarchus's understanding of justice that call for further reflection. His procedure presupposes, however, that Polemarchus is already more willing to listen to Socrates than Cephalus was. Polemarchus in fact immediately begins to distinguish himself from his father: whereas Cephalus had no interest in discussing justice, Polemarchus interrupts when the subject is raised (331d). What accounts for the difference between father and son?

Although Cephalus initially asked Socrates "to come to us . . . as to friends" (328d), he made no further mention of friends or friendship (*philia*). In fact, Cephalus's enduring selfishness, like the tyrannical passions of his youth, rules out genuine friendship. Socrates, however, reintroduces the subject of friendship when he challenges Cephalus's understanding of justice. In particular, he implies that being just involves not doing harm to one's friends (331c). Polemarchus vehemently endorses and in fact extends this principle: he excitedly swears by Zeus in affirming that "friends owe it to friends to do some good and nothing bad" (332a).

The latter remark suggests that Polemarchus's alliance with Socrates becomes possible because he, unlike Cephalus, is genuinely open to the relationship of friendship. In the dialogue's opening scene, Polemarchus is represented as the leader of a band of friends held together by the kindred desires of its members for pleasures of various kinds (cf. Aristotle, *Ethics*, 8.3). His desires, however, have been extended and politicized in a way that Cephalus's have not. Like his father, Polemarchus is moved primarily by the love of his own things. Unlike his father, however, his conception of that which is his own is broad enough to encompass a multitude of individuals not related to him by blood. In particular, his *eros* is more than narrowly corporeal: it is directed toward the shared experience of pleasures that are enjoyed in common by his band of friends as a whole, and it therefore moves him beyond the tightly circumscribed circle of exclusive self-interest represented by his father.

Polemarchus is noteworthy for his *thumos* as well as his relative erotic breadth. He feels strong ties to his fellow Athenians. He is what the Greeks called *kalos k'agathos*—literally, "noble and good"—a "gentleman" willing to stand up for his friends and his city. Polemarchus's gentlemanly attachment to his friends is the prephilosophic basis of his interest in justice. This kind of attachment or affection is also at the root of the unity of the polis. As his name suggests, Polemarchus views the distinctions between friend and enemy and war and peace as most fundamental in understanding human relations. The poet Simonides claims "that it is just to give each what is owed" (331e); it seems obvious to Polemarchus that "what is owed" means "what is fitting," and that what is fitting depends on whom one is dealing with. Specifically, friends deserve good things and nothing bad, whereas enemies deserve ills (332a-c). Polemarchus's courageous loyalty to his friends, which is best evidenced in the violent circumstances of his death, is a politically crucial virtue: a community whose members did not stand up for one another as friends could not long endure.

Never in the course of the *Republic* does Socrates challenge either the general definition of justice as giving each what is fitting or Polemarchus's intuition that being just to one's friends means doing some good and nothing bad to them. This fact suggests that in Socrates' view Polemarchus's intuition is a sound one. But Socrates does force Polemarchus to question who his friends are, why they are his friends, and what good it is that one does in being just to them. In exploring these questions, Socrates begins to inquire into the presuppositions of the polis.

From 332c to 334b Socrates focuses on what justice accomplishes. The upshot of this perplexing section is that it is unclear what the just man does or in what way justice is useful, at least during times of peace. What is worse, the just man, far from being a truth teller who returns deposits (331d), now appears to be a liar and a thief, a patently unjust lesson for which Socrates blames Homer, "for he [Homer] admires Autolycus ["Lone Wolf"], Odysseus' grandfather on his mother's side, and says he surpassed all men 'in stealing and in swearing [false] oaths' " (334a-b). How can we explain this shocking result?

In trying to pull Polemarchus further into the inquiry, Socrates himself seems to engage in Autolycan or Odyssean sleights-of-hand. Socrates' Odyssean shiftiness is especially evident in the task he sets for Polemarchus: to identify the art or *technē* of justice, by analogy with cookery and medicine (332c-d). Art or craft is the most obvious and the most common kind of knowledge: a *technē* may be defined as any procedure involving a number of steps that aims at a goal and is teachable. Such knowledge is in fact so obvious and so common that one may wonder whether all knowledge is not technical knowledge. Yet Polemarchus replies that "*if* the answer has to be consistent with what preceded," justice is the *technē* "that gives benefits and injuries to friends and enemies" (332d; my italics). Polemarchus's hesitation should give us pause as well: Is being just equivalent to possessing a certain kind of technical knowledge? The absurdity into which Socrates leads Polemarchus—namely, that the just man is a thief, because the best guard is also the best robber (334a-b)—seems to show that it is not. Put simply, any *technē* can be used justly or unjustly, the same way that whether a man is just or unjust is irrelevant to his ability to learn any given *technē*. This would also hold true for a hypothetical *technē* of justice. Many unjust men know that their actions are technically unjust; to be just, however, means to be *unwilling* to do injustice. Being just, in other words, involves a predisposition of the soul to choose just actions over unjust ones. To the extent that this predisposition involves knowledge, it is knowledge of the choiceworthy ends and of the life worth living, not technical knowledge of the means to achieve a given end. Hence, justice may involve technical knowledge—for example, the just distribution of resources may involve knowledge of economics—but is not reducible to technical knowledge.

To Thrasymachus, Socrates' polytropism is a mark of his injustice: Socrates refutes whatever anyone says in order to gratify his love of honor (336c). Is Socrates being unjust in his discussion with Polemarchus? The most we can say at this point is that Socratic education, unlike technical instruction, is not a matter of simply transferring knowledge from one soul to another—as, for example, by the "force-feeding" Thrasymachus offers Socrates at 345b. Indeed, Socrates resembles the thief Autolycus in one important respect: he teaches in part by *taking away* from his interlocutors unreflective opinions that impede their discovery of the truth.[1] One's ability to distinguish the give-and-take of Socratic discourse from fraud and theft perhaps depends ultimately on whether one values the quest for wisdom more than other pursuits. Thrasymachus, one should note, interprets Socrates' intentions in the light of his own strong love of honor (338a).

66

Polemarchus is unwilling to give up his definition of justice as helping friends and harming enemies, although he now admits that he does not know what being just specifically involves (334b). Having convinced Polemarchus that "helping" is a problematic notion, Socrates critically explores "friends and enemies" and "harming" in the remainder of their conversation (334b-36a).

Polemarchus explains that we are fond of those who seem good and useful and hate those who seem worthless; the former are our friends and the latter our enemies (334c). The *philia* that binds friends to one another is rooted in the desire for that which is good and useful for oneself. But Polemarchus, unlike Cephalus, is prepared to acknowledge that human beings make mistakes in distinguishing between what is and what merely seems to be the case, perhaps because he himself has just witnessed the transformation of the just man into his opposite, the thief. He is hence compelled to redefine friends and enemies in terms of what they are, not what they seem to be (334e-35a).

Polemarchus's admission of fallibility represents a turning point in his encounter with Socrates. Since he desires what *is* genuinely good and useful for himself and not merely what *seems* to be, Polemarchus must acknowledge the preeminent importance of a philosophical investigation of that in the light of which we can distinguish between genuine friends (good men) and enemies (worthless men), including in particular an investigation of the things worth striving for and the life worth living. Socrates has won an ally. If it is just to encourage critical, philosophical reflection, Socrates has done justice to Polemarchus as well.

The present discussion of friendship nonetheless calls into question the *philia* that manifests itself as patriotism and thereby holds together political community. To Cephalus, the basis of patriotism is convenience: Athens, for example, is a good place to make money or win fame (329e-30a). This view, which follows directly from natural selfishness or the love of one's own things, raises a vexing problem: Why may I not regard my fellow citizens as enemies, and my city's enemies as friends, whenever it seems to serve my own interests to do so? Put bluntly, Why be just? The internal coherence of Polemarchus's spirited patriotism—and, indeed, the enduring integrity of political community—depend on an adequate answer to this question.

Strikingly, the *Republic* has already begun to answer the question "Why be just?" on the level of dramatic action. Socrates' relationship with Polemarchus, which at the outset of the dialogue was characterized by a typically political mixture of force, persuasion, and desire, has now become a model of the kind of association that transcends convenience—the kind political community aspires to be. Before constructing the city-in-speech, Socrates and Polemarchus have founded a philosophic community, or *koinōnia*, in deed. They will "share in battle as partners [*koinōnein*]" in defending their common understanding of justice (335e), which now includes, despite Socrates' reference to "battle," a restriction against harming anyone (335d)—surely a prudent measure if one is ignorant of who one's friends and enemies really are. While this new partnership anticipates the Kallipolis in its subordination of spiritedness to intellect, it is an actual community of discourse as opposed to an imaginary regime. Most important, the members of this community understand that its roots lie not in an accidental confluence of desires but in the unquestionable desirability of further philosophic inquiry into that which is, in the broadest sense, desirable. Justice, it seems, inheres in the activity of philosophy itself.

THRASYMACHUS AND THE CHALLENGE OF SOPHISTRY

Thrasymachus's Charge   Like Polemarchus, Thrasymachus enters the conversation by way of interruption. His sudden assault on Socrates (336b*ff*) makes the connection between Socratic philosophizing and justice an explicit topic of debate. Like Socrates' public accusers, Thrasymachus sets forth an indictment and demands punishment (337d). As they will at his trial, Socrates' friends agree to pay any fine he may incur (cf. *Apology*, 38b), and Polemarchus is at one point said to "witness" for him (340a). Yet Socrates' ironic fearfulness (336b-e) lends comic overtones to an intrinsically serious discussion.

These dramatic clues suggest that the philosophic and political issues at stake in both the *Clouds* and the *Apology* inform the present context as well.

In every important respect, Thrasymachus challenges the conception of philosophy that emerges from Socrates' discussion with Polemarchus. Thrasymachus accuses Socrates of injustice and bad philosophizing. Socrates, he asserts, acts as if his refutative style of discourse will lead to philosophic insight, but his speech is at bottom purely combative or eristic. Apart from all appearances, Socratic discussion is actually more like war than peaceful partnership, and it has nothing to do with the attainment of knowledge. Socrates ironically claims that knowledge of justice is worth more than gold, but his real aim is victory in argument (336e-37a). And in any case, refutative discourse will never yield knowledge. To really know what justice is, one must make a clear and precise claim about its nature—something Socrates is never willing to do about any subject (336b-d).

Thrasymachus is no stranger to the practice of eristic rhetoric: he clearly believes that he possesses knowledge of justice *and* that this knowledge guarantees for him the honor of defeating Socrates in the rhetorical equivalent of hand-to-hand combat (338a, 341b). Such a victory would both gratify his own desire to win repute and be good for his business as a teacher of political and legal persuasion. Thrasymachus says Socrates and Polemarchus are fools (336c): he relishes what he perceives to be the contrast between himself, a man who knows what is good and how to get it all—money, honor, and wisdom—and Socrates, a poor dope who is about to be disgraced.

Is Thrasymachus's self-understanding internally coherent? In particular, if Socrates' ostensibly warlike disposition is at odds with the quest for and possession of wisdom, as Thrasymachus implies, must not the same be true of Thrasymachus? Socrates suggests as much by portraying his rival as a threat both to peaceful partnerships and to logos or reasonable speech itself. When the men who wish to hear the argument (logos) can no longer restrain him, Thrasymachus interrupts Socrates and Polemarchus like a "wild beast" (336b). Wild beasts, we may note, are fit for neither philosophic nor political community because they are savage and lack the capacity for reasonable speech about common affairs such as justice and injustice (cf. Aristotle, *Politics*, 1253a7-18). Socrates later adds that Thrasymachus, like the mythical wolf, was almost able to render him "voiceless" (336d; cf. Bloom 1968, 444*n*30). Perhaps it is Thrasymachus, not Socrates, who most resembles Autolycus, the lone wolf.

Socrates' comments anticipate the seemingly contradictory quality of Thrasymachus's words and deeds: Thrasymachus defines justice as injustice, since it is "nothing other than the advantage of the stronger" (338c), and in so doing he makes a speech that somehow brings logos to a standstill. But Thrasymachus, a "surprising man" (337b), is proud of his boldly paradoxical teaching. While Cephalus is unconsciously Cyclopean in his enslavement to his own body, his blindness to the sacred, and his exclusive concern for his own things, Thrasymachus is explicitly so in his willingness to debunk justice. In particular, Thrasymachus is happy to defend the claim that might makes right because he fancies himself to be one of "the stronger" and views Socrates as a "nobody" or "nonentity" (*ouden*, 341c). Thrasymachus's puffery is ironically reminiscent of Polyphemus's boasting (see esp. *Odyssey*, 9.366, where Odysseus cleverly tells Polyphemus his name is *Outis*, "Nobody"). Socrates, in turn, comically deflates Thrasymachus's blustery pretensions by feigning excessive fear. By suggesting that he is not afraid of Thrasymachus on any level, Socrates invites us to ask how Socratic courage compares with Thrasymachean boldness.

Socrates is interested in conversations like the present one because he learns from them (337d, 338b). How so? Socrates' search for the best life involves a commitment to the philosophic life that is based not on knowledge but on "belief" or "supposition" (337e). Socrates further supposes that the best way to test his beliefs is directly to expose himself to the challenges represented by other human beings leading other lives. His procedure in this regard is intellectually more honest and courageous than that of the many sophists (and professors!) who choose to remain safely within the circle of their disciples and likeminded colleagues. Indeed, the most forceful challenges are potentially the most revealing, regardless of the outcome. Just as Socrates' inability to draw Cephalus into a critical discussion helped to expose the limits of philosophic discourse, he will have learned something even if Thrasymachus fails to "teach him a lesson."

Cephalus implied that men are just only out of fear of the gods' superior strength. Thrasymachus extends this insight and applies it to the polis: "in every city the same thing is just, the advantage of the established ruling body" (339a). In other words, those with political power define *nomos*, the measure of justice, in a way that serves their own advantage but not that of the ruled. Thrasymachus further implies that different sorts of regimes will define justice in different ways, because the advantage of each kind of ruling group is opposed to that of the others. Thrasymachus's deconstruction of *nomos* leads to the conclusion that politics is domination. By stripping away the veneer of *nomos*, Thrasymachus exposes what he takes to be an irreducible conflict of private interests on the level of *phusis*. Even the interests of the rulers (if a number hold power) conflict, as Thrasymachus's subsequent praise of tyranny as perfect injustice makes clear (344a-c). Because this conflict is absolutely fundamental, it cannot be settled by logos. Rhetorical speech is instrumental in concealing the conflict, but philosophic inquiry cannot resolve it. The polis, like the arena of foreign relations, is in effect a war zone in which one's friends are defined as those with whom it is temporarily convenient to band together for the sake of plundering others. If civil war does not actually break out, it is because some men are restrained by fear (344c), while others are simpletons who fail to appreciate that being just is beneficial to those in power but detrimental to themselves (343a*ff*).

It is now clear why Socrates suggested that Thrasymachus was hostile to logos in general and philosophic discourse in particular. Thrasymachus takes it for granted that human beings are characterized by *pleonexia*, the unlimited desire always "to have more" (*pleon echein*) of a good thing than one currently has, and to have more than others as well. *Pleonexia* is not restricted to wealth, although Thrasymachus, who has a high opinion of wealth (see 336e, 344e-45a), stresses that the unjust man "gets more than" (*pleonektein*) the just man by cheating on his taxes, plundering public funds, and the like (343d*ff*). More important than what is desired, however, is Thrasymachus's assumption that each conflicts with all in pursuing his own advantage. This assumption comprehensively undermines discourse about questions of worth, since anyone who understands his own advantage will speak in a way that is helpful to himself but harmful to others whenever he perceives his advantage to be at stake. As Thrasymachus points out, such perceptions are decisive with regard to speech about justice; debate about what is good or bad and noble or base will be similarly distorted by each person's consideration of his own self-interest. Consequently, what passes for reasonable speech about these things is really self-serving rhetoric. Whether the context is political or philosophical, logos cannot be expected to arrive at the truth about what is worthwhile or worthless, since speech about these things reflects the private interests of the speaker. And in any case, the truth would be irrelevant to intelligent people, whose primary concern is to increase their own advantage.

The seeming consistency of the preceding reflections masks Thrasymachus's deeply paradoxical nature. On the one hand, he prides himself on his intelligent, clear, and precise speech about justice and injustice; on the other, his account of the relationship between speech and personal advantage undercuts the theoretical validity of any such public speech, including his own account. One could say that Thrasymachus, whose *erōs* extends beyond the purely private domain of the body to wisdom and the honor the wise deserve, conceals from himself the difference between himself and Cephalus. Socrates refutes Thrasymachus by exploiting the aforementioned paradox and thus reminding him of his non-Cephalanean nature. Socrates' effect on Thrasymachus is liberating—he frees him to pursue his own education, something of which Cephalus is wholly incapable.

Socratic Justice: The Strength of Logos   In order to "tame" Thrasymachus and rescue the logos from silence—a heroic task, to be sure—Socrates must convince Thrasymachus that it is to *everyone's* advantage to discover the truth about the just and the advantageous. Such a recognition implies that one can know, or be mistaken about, what is advantageous for oneself. Thrasymachus readily admits as much (339c); after all, the rhetorical skill he peddles is designed to help men avoid making mistakes in obtaining their advantage. The importance of this crucial admission is underscored by the brief debate between Polemarchus and Cleitophon, who argues for a radical sort of relativism that rules out mistakes of the sort Socrates has in mind: "the advantage of the stronger is what the stronger *believes* to be his advantage" (340b; my italics). Having once spoken, Cleitophon is never heard from again in the *Republic*. His silence is dramatically appropriate, because he has nothing to contribute to the inquiry: his extreme relativism obliterates the distinction between seeming and being with regard to questions of worth. Like Cephalus, he is not open to the possibility that he may be mistaken about the most important things. He too is beyond the saving powers of philosophy.[2]

Thrasymachus dissociates himself from Cleitophon, and in fact he exhibits a robust intellectual optimism in implying that he possesses and teaches a *technē* of the advantageous that can be articulated with clarity and precision, like the arts of medicine, calculation, and grammar—a triad that tellingly emphasizes bodily health, wealth, and the formation of speeches (340d-e). The ruler in the precise sense, he asserts, does not make mistakes, "and not making mistakes, he sets down what is best for himself" (341a).

At issue, however, is precisely what the art of rule accomplishes. Socrates' analogies for political rule are medicine and piloting (cf. 332c-e). Thrasymachus's is shepherding: political rule exists for the purpose of fleecing human beings. Socrates' later claim that the "true shepherd" looks only to the advantage of his sheep (345c-d) is irrelevant and could even be used in defense of tyranny. The shepherd seeks to make his sheep good for fleecing and eating—that is, fat and woolly. So too the true butcher looks to the good of the meat qua meat in cutting it up and seasoning it. The issue, however, is whether the ruler should treat the ruled as if they were meat- and wool-producing animals, or in some other way.

The present discussion, as Socrates points out, is really about the best way of life (344d-e, 352d), about which he and Thrasymachus fundamentally disagree. Thrasymachus argues that the man who would be perfectly happy must overturn the entire structure of political community, subverting "what is sacred and profane, private and public, not bit by bit, but all at once" (344a). The issue of the best way of life is politically the most radical issue of all, and potentially the most divisive (cf. *Euthyphro*, 7c-d). It cannot adequately be framed in terms of *technē*, because it is prior to art: our understanding of the life or lives most worth living determines how we use the arts and guides our relations of social cooperation.

Socrates' conception of philosophic discourse also includes an idea of justice that he attempts to impress on his adversary: if I am ignorant, he tells Thrasymachus, then it is fitting for me to learn (337d). In the end, Socrates dramatically demonstrates the superior strength of justice by forcing the champion of injustice blushingly to concede his ignorance, and by thus giving him what is fitting: a lesson in justice (350d). Specifically, Socrates compels Thrasymachus to admit that knowledge implies unanimity among knowers with regard to that which is known (349e-50c). Knowledge, it turns out, is something advantageous that *can* be shared or held in common. Indeed, if it cannot be shared, it is presumably not knowledge. In this specific sense there is justice among knowers: knowers do not try to get the better of one another with regard to their common knowledge. Thus if Thrasymachus really possessed knowledge of the advantageous, he would not try to get the better in argument of everyone else without exception, since he would not dispute with those who possess this same knowledge. Conversely, since Thrasymachus implies that discussion of the advantageous is always equivalent to war, it follows that he does not possess, or is at least unwilling to teach, the knowledge he claims to teach. He blushes because Socrates manages to make him look like an ignoramus who unjustly tries to cheat others out of their money in exchange for worthless teaching. Socrates, by comparison, appears wise and just in offering Thrasymachus a valuable lesson for free.

Thrasymachus really does learn from Socrates, for he comes to recognize that he esteems the truth, as well as the honor that derives from being able to articulate the truth, far more than his account suggests, and in a way that directly conflicts with what he asserts to be his own advantage. Thrasymachus's explicit praise of injustice should itself serve his own interests as he understands them, but instead Socrates has easily shown that it hinders these interests: only a fool would pay for lessons with a teacher who argues against the possibility of his own claim to deliver knowledge and who prides himself on being a cheat (349b-50d). Thrasymachus's explanation of the self-serving nature of speech about the just and the advantageous does not explain his own motives in publicly setting forth the explanation itself. One might infer that Thrasymachus is not very clever, but the fact that he remains and continues to attend to the discussion even after he has been bested by Socrates suggests that he himself draws a different conclusion—namely, that he was mistaken about the nature of the advantageous, particularly about the possibility and desirability of the quest for knowledge of the good. Although his interpretation of human life is in many ways a sophisticated expansion of Cephalus's, Thrasymachus ultimately proves superior to Cephalus because he is attracted not only to money but also to wisdom and the honor associated with wisdom. Thrasymachus's pride in his own intelligence, like Polemarchus's attachment to his friends, finally allows Socrates to win him over: he becomes Socrates' "friend," and at one point he even reminds Socrates that the assembled company has come "to listen to arguments [*logoi*]," not "to look for fool's gold" (498c-d, 450b).

SPIRITEDNESS AND PHILOSOPHY

Philosophy in certain respects resembles both peace and war. Philosophy requires dialogue and presupposes justice in speaking and listening, inasmuch as the activity of philosophic dialogue rests on the possibility of sharing knowledge in partnership with others. Socrates' conversion of Thrasymachus into a friend of philosophy dramatically demonstrates this possibility, and thus responds to Aristophanes' doubts about the difference between logos and self-serving noise. By the same token, Socrates' peaceful conversion of Thrasymachus represents the overcoming of closed, Cephalanean *erōs*. Yet the quest for wisdom is also warlike in that it thrives on challenge and languishes in its absence. The philosopher without *thumos*—the philosopher who does not relish the clash of ideas—is no philosopher at all. In the speeches and deeds of Socrates, book 1 dramatically exhibits the relationship between *thumos* and self-restraint and the qualities of courage and justice that are essential to a philosophic education.

Book 1 also highlights the problematic character of *thumos*. While Polemarchus and Thrasymachus are friends of philosophy, they are not philosophers. Furthermore, *thumos* seems to be naturally allied with the love of honor and the love of victory for its own sake. To what extent can the ambition of the most highly spirited individual be directed toward the achievement of wisdom? With this question in mind, we turn to Socrates' encounter with Glaucon.

7

Beginning Anew: Socratic Mythmaking and Philosophic Pedagogy

While book 1 exhibits the birth of philosophic discourse, Socrates admits that he has merely set the table for more discussion about the nature of the soul and the life worth living (354a-c). Book 1 especially underscores the problem of the desirability of philosophy. Why is the philosophic life—let alone the just but nonphilosophic life—preferable to the unjust life of complete erotic liberation? Socrates has not yet settled this issue, since Thrasymachus is by his own standards insufficiently unjust. He makes his living as a teacher of persuasive speech, and so must speak in such a way as to attract students. He is therefore weak, or bound by *nomos*, in a way that the tyrant apparently is not. Could Socrates defend the just life in general, or the philosophic life in particular, against a more completely unjust opponent?

The latter question would not have been pursued if Glaucon, "always most courageous in everything," had not reformulated Thrasymachus's defense of injustice and compelled Socrates to continue the discussion (357a; cf. 368c). Glaucon now requests an account of the power of justice in the soul. Adeimantus subsequently enlarges Socrates' task by showing that to refute his brother's argument one must criticize the whole mythical component of the Greek religious tradition. Homer and Hesiod were the most influential educators of Greece, since their myths provided the first great paradigms of human virtue and vice and of man's proper relationship with the gods. Yet, as Adeimantus argues, the poeticoreligious tradition they founded is politically inadequate insofar as it ultimately fails to produce citizens inclined to choose justice over injustice. Indeed, Adeimantus locates in the poeticoreligious tradition itself the roots of post-traditional Athenian corruption. Since this tradition has already informed the opinions and desires of Socrates' companions, Socrates must attempt to reeducate them. In brief, he must attempt to undo much of what the mythical orthodoxy of the polis has already accomplished.

In response to the requests of Glaucon and Adeimantus, Socrates hits upon the idea of imaginatively refounding political community itself. In so doing, Socrates tells a myth—or, more accurately, a series of myths about successive cities. I call these "myths" not only because they are stories designed to supplant the traditional myths of the poets in content and pedagogic effect, but also because in them we enter a realm of fantasy, in which what is envisioned is in crucial respects both humanly impossible and undesirable. Yet Socrates' attitude toward these myths is complex and by no means wholly ironic, because the myths highlight the contradictory nature of the human soul and so the inherently paradoxical nature of education. Furthermore, the construction of a city-in-speech is a task well-suited to the specific pedagogical requirements of the present conversation. Socrates' main concern is to turn his companions toward justice and philosophy. His project nicely serves this aim, for to reconstruct the bonds of *nomos* that bind a political community together is to reenact the shaping of one's own soul.

In general, the impossible and humanly deficient character of the City of Pigs, the City of Adeimantus, and the Kallipolis is rooted in their unrealistic treatment of *erōs*. By involving his companions in the activity of constructing these cities-in-speech, however, Socrates deals quite subtly with the matter of *their erōs* and potential for injustice. Far from being simply restricted, for example, Glaucon's "conventional" desires find expression in the Feverish City that grows out of the

City of Pigs. This city mirrors the overheated condition both of Glaucon's soul and of the Athenian community that has shaped his character. In helping Socrates to purge the Feverish City of its sickness, Glaucon and his companions will indirectly be criticizing themselves—a process made more effective by their simultaneous detachment, as "legislators," from the vices they criticize, and attachment, as founding fathers or poets, to the mythical education they devise.

In this and the following chapter I explore both the political and philosophical ambiguities of Socrates' mythical cities and the pedagogical virtues of their construction. Let us begin with the problem of *erōs* as presented by the characters of Glaucon and Adeimantus.

GLAUCON AND THE TYRANNY OF DESIRE

Because Glaucon attempts to improve upon the sophist's conception of perfect injustice, Socrates implies he is Thrasymachus's child (368a; cf. Bloom 1968, 448*n*21). Yet Glaucon also has a special relationship with Socrates. He alone accompanied Socrates to the Piraeus, and he had no qualms about speaking for his companion when Polemarchus demanded that they stay. He is eager to listen to Socrates on the subject of the best men, and initially he comes forward as his ally in the argument against Thrasymachus (347a-e).

As in the dialogue's opening scene, it seems that a special concern for Glaucon motivates Socrates to stay and talk. Socrates' attachment to Glaucon may have something to do with his special potential for philosophic education, although we shall have reason to question the extent to which even Glaucon is capable of pursuing philosophy. An interesting piece of evidence with regard to both Socrates' motives and Glaucon's philosophic potential is Xenophon's claim that, as a favor to Plato, Socrates tried to check Glaucon's headstrong appetite for political power and honor (*Memorabilia*, 3.6). Socrates' decision to yield to Polemarchus and remain in the Piraeus may be rooted in loyalty to a friend. In any case, Glaucon's loyalty to Socrates is by no means automatic; it is, rather, the reflective allegiance of a young man whose high spirits and aristocratic breeding have given him an intense desire to live the best and most outstanding life.

Socrates is aware that Glaucon has arrived at a crossroads. Although Glaucon defends Thrasymachean boldness, his own "most courageous" character reflects an unstable mixture of political and philosophical courage. The word for courage is *andreia*, literally "manliness," for *andres* are adult male members of a political community. Glaucon respects the manly civic virtues that sustain political community, but he is ready—especially after having been stirred up by Thrasymachus—to abandon them unless they can be shown to be conducive to the best life. Intellectually and morally, Glaucon cannot remain where he is. Poised between *nomos* and critical reflection, he will inevitably move toward either sophistical injustice or philosophically grounded justice.

Why does Socrates imply that Glaucon is more philosophically courageous than Thrasymachus? The answer lies in each man's attitude toward logos. Whereas Thrasymachus's speech paradoxically entailed the impossibility of philosophic discourse about the advantageous, the just, and the noble—Glaucon appropriately remarks that he has been "talked deaf by Thrasymachus" (358c)—Glaucon restates the case for injustice in a way that explicitly invites further inquiry. It is crucial to notice, however, that if Socratic discourse cannot move us beyond the impasses into which critical reflection on *nomos* may lead us, philosophic courage will turn out to be indistinguishable in practice from sophistic, politically destructive rashness. If philosophy cannot adequately defend justice, Glaucon will choose a life of cleverly disguised tyranny.

Glaucon suggests that Socrates, like a charmer of poisonous snakes, has calmed the serpent Thrasymachus with mere rhetoric and thereby cast a spell that will soon wear off (358b). Glaucon will break this spell by sharpening Thrasymachus's argument: "the extreme of injustice is to seem to be just when one is not" (361a). His speech falls into three parts: an account of the nature and origin of justice (358e-59b), the Myth of Gyges' Ring (359b-60d), and a comparison of the just life and the unjust life (360e-62c). Glaucon's attribution of his argument to "the many" (358a) is meant to veil its reflection of his own desires, but it also indicates his uncertainty about its persuasiveness. It will be up to Socrates to provide Glaucon with an effective antidote to the philosophically and politically venomous praise of injustice (cf. Derrida, 118*ff*).

Glaucon first claims that justice is laborious and harsh, and therefore undesirable in itself but useful for its wages and the good repute that follows from it (358a). But since the good consequences of justice can be obtained through injustice, which is easy for the few "real men" whose outstanding manliness makes them capable of it, justice is in no way desirable for those who are unimpeded by a "want of vigor" (359a-b; cf. 361b). Both the weak many and the manly few agree that getting away with injustice is by nature best, and being wronged without taking revenge is worst. By nature, men are characterized by *pleonexia*; *nomos*, however, demands that men "honor equality" (359c). Because the many fall short of the best and fear the worst, they alone agree to follow the middle path of neither doing nor suffering injustice. *Nomos* is thus determined by the weak, not the strong, as Thrasymachus had argued. Justice is therefore best by convention but is by nature strictly mediocre: nature itself sanctions injustice for those who can do it.

The Myth of Gyges' Ring, which illustrates the spiritedness of the "real man" and provides a detailed erotic justification for injustice, is on one level a literary register of Glaucon's psyche. Yet this tale also contains critical depths that come to light when its symbolic elements are seen in connection with the mythical structure of the *Republic*.

Gyges' unnamed ancestor is a shepherd of the ruler of Lydia. His barbarian origins and lowly vocation perhaps reflect Glaucon's pessimism about the possibility of a kind of politics that is distinct from the mastery of unfree subjects: fattening and fleecing sheep was a political analogy for Thrasymachus as well. The great thunderstorm and the earthquake that split open the ground are harbingers of the violence and subsequent upheaval that will take place in the political cosmos after the shepherd's discovery of the ring. This suggestion of violent, cosmic disruption is strengthened by the shepherd's descent into Hades and discovery of an unnaturally large, naked corpse inside a bronze horse. The deceptive, politically destructive power of the ring is reflected in the huge horse, which is reminiscent of the famous device, contrived by Odysseus, the master of disguises, with which the Greeks insinuated themselves into the city of Troy and then annihilated it from within.

The shepherd's outstanding characteristic is fearless inquisitiveness, a morally ambiguous, Odyssean quality shared also by Glaucon and Socrates. In motive and action, the shepherd's journey into the underworld parallels Socrates' trip to the Piraeus: when the chasm opened at his feet, "he saw it, wondered at it, and went down" (359d). But Glaucon's tale directly challenges Socratic philosophizing in its implication that one's initiation into the "Mysteries" of perfect injustice, as opposed to philosophy, makes possible the ascent to the best life. This initiation, represented in the myth by the frightful act of robbing a giant corpse while in a dark and strange region that is guarded by fearsome gods, requires boldness of heroic proportions. The shepherd's seizure of tyrannical power in Lydia follows easily from this critical theft—a deed few humans would have the nerve to accomplish.

Both horse and ring are technical artifacts. Their materials anticipate the metals with which the citizens' souls are said to be mixed in the Noble Lie, gold being the highest ranking and bronze the lowest (415a). Like Thrasymachus's *technē* of rule, the ring is an artificial device that substitutes for a gold or noble nature, as well as for the philosophical education that perfects such natures in the Kallipolis: the ring's possessor can attain political rule even if his soul is of the basest metal.

The soul is in fact conspicuously absent in Glaucon's tale. There is in particular no need critically to examine one's life: for the ring-bearer, the unexamined life is unquestionably worth living. The bare corpse, like Euripides' Polyphemus, is a massive symbol of "naked" bodily *erōs*. Plato plays here on the connection between clothing and convention (cf. 452b*ff*): the ring makes it unnecessary to cloak or constrain one's natural *erōs* in any of the ways convention prescribes. The corpse's hugeness suggests complete erotic fulfillment: with the power the ring confers, one's desires are free to grow as large and strong as possible. Its dimensions also seem to bespeak a life that exceeds the fitting proportions of human political existence—a life, Glaucon later indicates, that is suitable for gods (360c).

Glaucon ascribes to the many the notions of erotic satisfaction and of the good life represented in the ring tale, but Cephalus has already articulated the same opinion. This point is underscored by the mechanics of the ring, which works only when its collet is turned inward. Inwardness in this context is an image of exclusive self-obsession and purely private satisfaction. The soul of the ring-bearer takes on the shape of the band of gold: by enclosing itself within the circle of its own untutored passions—passions that are not all strictly bodily but are well represented by the privacy and immediacy of the body—it cuts itself off from the educative influence of that which lies above or beyond it. Seen in this light, the erotic liberation Glaucon praises is actually a kind of psychic bondage. The ring seems at home in the domain of dead souls.

The passions unleashed by the ring include Cephalus's most tyrannical "mad master": the shepherd's first unjust act after obtaining the ring is adultery with the king's wife. Glaucon's ruling passion, however, is for the honor that is accorded preeminent men, as is clear from his account of the ring's benefits. The shepherd uses adultery to guarantee the queen's complicity in murder. Furthermore, honor is first and foremost in Glaucon's list of the goods secured by perfect injustice: "First, he [the unjust man] rules in the city . . . then he takes in marriage from whatever station he wants," and "when he enters contests . . . he wins" (362b).

Despite their differences, Glaucon and Cephalus agree about the things men deem best: money, sexual pleasure, honor, and power. Most striking in this connection is Glaucon's remark that the man who steals, rapes, and slays at will acts "as an equal to a god among humans" (360b-c). Everyone, Glaucon argues, would behave in the same way if given the mythical ring, for the just secretly agree with the unjust that the life of full-blown erotic liberty is the most divine existence. Later Glaucon confirms Cephalus's suggestion that the gods can be bribed: the unjust man is dearer to the gods than the just man because his rich votive offerings are "far better" (362c). In short, humans look to the gods as paradigms of injustice. Glaucon's speech thus reopens the issue of the sacred and sets the stage for Adeimantus's subsequent criticisms of the originators of these paradigms, the poets.

A BROTHER'S APOLOGY

"Let a man stand by his brother," says Socrates when Adeimantus first pipes up (362d). Glaucon and Adeimantus are a natural pair, with different yet perhaps complementary qualities of soul. Whereas Glaucon is strongly attracted to injustice, Adeimantus is characterized by moral delicacy. Adeimantus represents what Glaucon needs: he is someone, Plato puns, who *would* "be so adamant [*adamantinos*] as to stick by justice" even if he possessed Gyges' ring (360b). He is not insensitive to the goods at which injustice aims, but he is disgusted by baseness. For this reason, his attack on those who "vulgarly" turn the powers of justice and injustice "upside down" (367a) is colored by moral indignation.

Adeimantus "stands by his brother" in that he shifts the blame for Glaucon's attraction to injustice to the poeticoreligious tradition that has educated them both. He is particularly indignant because the speeches of the many and of their teachers, the poets, corrupt the young, especially those who, like Glaucon, "have good natures and have the capacity, as it were, to fly to all the things that are said and gather from them what sort of man one should be" (365a).

Adeimantus begins by criticizing the way in which fathers and poets praise justice not for itself but for the goods that follow from being reputed to be just (362e-63e). No value is thereby attached actually to being just. Indeed, Adeimantus turns Aristophanes' central accusation against Socrates back on the poets themselves: the poets, even in attempting to defend justice, fail to distinguish that which is high and sacred from that which is low and profane. In explaining our relations with the gods in commercial terms, Cephalus and Glaucon were merely repeating the teaching of ancient authorities: starting with Homer and Hesiod, the poets maintain that the reputation of justice brings "wages" from the gods. Furthermore, Greeks are instructed in the

Eleusinian Mysteries that in the afterlife, as Adeimantus says with disdain, "the finest wage of virtue is an eternal drunk" (363c-d; cf. Bloom 1968, 447*n*10).

Against injustice, the poets can allege only distant penalties after death. These penalties, however, can be avoided by propitiating the gods with sacrifices and offerings, as the gods' spokesmen maintain (366a-b). In addition, poets and nonpoets alike agree that the gods are indifferent to the fate of good men. If men undergo religious initiations and engage in sacrifice, it is only because they have been taught by the likes of Homer himself that the gods are susceptible to bribery. Finally, the most eminent poets concur with Glaucon regarding the laboriousness of justice and the ease and profitability of injustice. In general, men pay lip service to justice while they honor and praise the unjust (363e-65a).

Adeimantus in effect urges Socrates not to be angry with Glaucon, for "after all that has been said, by what device . . . will a man who has some power—of soul, money, body, or family—be made willing to honor justice and not laugh when he hears it praised?" (366b-c). Intelligent young men will conclude from the speeches of the many and the eminent that the greatest injustice, disguised (as in the Cave) by "a shadow-painting of virtue," is preferable to justice (365c). Most important, they will reason that the gods are either nonexistent or indifferent to human affairs, or that they are such as *nomos* and the poets deem them to be ("for we know of them or have heard of them from nowhere else")—that is, "such as to be persuaded and perverted by sacrifice, soothing vows, and votive offerings" (365e). In these circumstances it is only to be expected that no one is willingly just, "except for someone who from a divine nature cannot stand doing injustice"—like Adeimantus himself—"or who has gained knowledge and keeps away from injustice" (366c).

Adeimantus lays out Socrates' task with maximum clarity. In the *Clouds* Socrates was depicted as a corrupter of traditional belief and a champion of injustice. In the *Republic* Adeimantus brings to light the incoherence of civic religion—which provides mythical models of great injustice and equates ritual obeisance with bribery even while stressing justice—and asks Socrates to right what the tradition itself has vulgarly inverted. The task with which Plato's brothers charge Socrates is nothing less than to explicate the powers and effects of justice and injustice in the soul—and so, using logos as medicine for the soul, to make intelligent and spirited young men like Glaucon, whom nature's very gifts have left singularly vulnerable to the attractions of injustice, "willing to honor justice."

Socrates' Godsend

Socrates twice claims that it is impossible for him adequately to defend justice (362d, 368b). In nevertheless asserting that it would be impious of him not at least to try (368b), he reminds us that his philosophic activity is inseparable from a deep appreciation of the sacred. It is precisely the sanctity of things divine that is at issue here, for the many and the eminent have slandered the gods by depicting them as models of injustice (cf. *Euthyphro*, 6a).

With the encouragement of his companions, Socrates launches the radical inquiry that occupies the next five books. His decision to found a city-in-speech makes sense in the light of Adeimantus's request, for to comply with this request is in effect critically to reconstruct *nomos* from its very beginnings: as Adeimantus observes, "beginning with the heroes [the founders of cities] at the beginning [*ex archēs*] . . . there is not one who has ever blamed injustice or praised justice other than for the reputations, honors, and gifts that come from them" (366e). An *archē* may be an "origin" and "ruling power" as well as a "beginning." Socrates proposes what amounts to a philosophic archaeology of the polis as well as the soul. In originating a political community, Socrates suggests, he and his companions will attempt to confront the *archai* of human life in all the preceding senses. By imaginatively reenacting the generation of a political tradition from its natural beginnings, they will try to strip away many sedimented layers of *nomos* in order to expose the bedrock of *phusis*, and then to account for the accretion of custom and convention on this foundation.

As promising as this project sounds, it is not the one in which Socrates actually engages. As in the *Clouds*, Socrates presents us in the course of constructing the city-in-speech with a distorted picture of human nature, a picture that blurs the distinction between human beings and animals.

Socrates' methodology is partly responsible for the latter distortion. The guiding principle of Socrates' philosophic archaeology is provided by a theoretically tentative "godsend" (*hermaion*: literally, a "gift of Hermes")—namely, the supposition that the soul and the city may be composed of the same "letters" or elements (368c-d). Socrates later admits that his method is inadequate to the understanding of the soul (435c-d). In particular, the central philosophical premise of his godsend is doubtful. If the soul is composed of letterlike elements, it is itself—or it at least possesses—a complex formal structure, the knowledge of which is knowledge of the soul. To acquire this knowledge, one need only "read" these letters; it is easy to give a logos of the soul if the soul is itself a kind of word or set of words. But formal structures—especially if the forms in question are unchanging Ideas, as Socrates later argues—are lifeless and motionless, whereas the human soul is alive and changing. Unlike the Ideas on the one hand, and the simpler souls of animals on the other, human souls—at least those that have not been hardened by age or narrowness of vision—are elastic and polymorphic; they never fully *are* but are at best always striving, searching, and coming-to-be. The human soul is itself polytropic: it has the capacity to take on many different looks, and so it can be "read" in many different and even contradictory ways. Precisely insofar as the soul is erotic, it is always in motion, in ways that disclose its openness or responsiveness to the contexts within which it moves. Indeed, our reading of the *Republic* has already suggested that this openness, and the sense of incompleteness that accompanies it, is the most distinctive feature of our humanity. Socrates' godsend therefore obscures the erotic character of the soul, even as it appears to increase the ease of giving a logos of the soul.

Socrates' reference to Hermes nonetheless points hopefully toward the possible pedagogic instrumentality of the city-in-speech. Hermes' gift-giving plays an important role in Homer's *Odyssey*: the divine messenger saves the day when he forewarns Odysseus that Circe has turned his crew into pigs, and provides him with an antidote to her foul magic in the form of a root with protective powers. The porcine form of Odysseus's companions is an image of their debased souls, for prior to Circe's sorcery they had immersed themselves in immediate pleasures and lost all desire or thought for their homeland (*Odyssey*, 10.234-36). Perhaps by means of the present interpretive godsend, Socrates will be able similarly to rescue his own companions from the dehumanizing tyranny of untutored, unbridled *erōs*.

Odysseus was unable to go straight home after leaving Circe: he was compelled first to visit Calypso's isle of Ogugia and then to sojourn on Scheria among the Phaeacians. Similarly, the City of Pigs is just the beginning of a philosophic journey in which the City of Adeimantus and the Kallipolis are represented as mythical analogues of Ogugia and Scheria. Far from being final destinations, the cities of Plato's brothers are no more than way-stations along the homeward road.

Socrates suggests in discussing the Good that Glaucon would be unable to follow him in the fullest explanation of his opinion (506e-507a). If it is troubling to think that none of Odysseus's shipmates returned home, it may yet be the case that some of Plato's readers will be able to accompany Socrates in his philosophic homecoming still further than his companions.

CHARTING OUR COURSE: THE CITY OF PIGS AND THE FEVERISH CITY

Like Odysseus and his crew, Socrates and his companions must steer clear of more than one form of psychic danger. The first two cities they construct are opposing extremes, between which the best city must be sought. The City of Pigs and the souls of its inhabitants are "healthy" or well-ordered, but radically deficient in *erōs* and *thumos* and so incompletely human; the Feverish City, which typifies existing cities, is fully human but disordered or "feverish" in its erotic and spirited character. The best city—the city on which Socrates and the others subsequently set their sights—may be abstractly envisioned as a whole that combines the health of the first city with the humanity of the second. The best city would somehow combine *erōs* with good order and moderation: it would be both philosophical and just. Yet the radical opposition between the City of Pigs and the Feverish City calls into question the theoretical coherence, let alone the human possibility, of any such middle ground. The first two cities thus clarify the goal at which Socrates aims, while warning that the "healthy" city may purchase justice at the cost of deforming that which is most distinctively human.

According to Socrates, political community comes into being "because each of us isn't self-sufficient but is in need of much" (369b). By allowing our needs to "make a city in speech from the beginning" (369c), it would appear to be possible to isolate those elements of political community that are rooted in *phusis*, understood as natural necessity. Because the first city will be structured in accordance with natural necessity alone (the words *need* and *necessity* recur frequently in these pages), its order will be natural, not conventional. *Phusis* is thus ostensibly visible in the first city in two respects: the primordial needs that bring humans together, and the ways in which nature in general has provided for these needs.

While Socrates takes up the topic of poetry later in book 2, it is important to note that his critical reconstruction of the Greek poetic tradition in fact begins with the first city. The first city is Socrates' modification of Hesiod's fabled Golden Age, the Greek equivalent of the Garden of Eden in which the earliest humans are supported by nature's superabundance.[1] The first city differs from the Golden Age and the Garden of Eden in that in it humans must labor to live. Its mythical character is nonetheless evident in nature's extraordinary providence, whereby the community is provided with appropriate quantities of various workers suited to perform each necessary task.

The first city meets man's basic need for food, shelter, and clothing; it exists for the sake of material exchange (371b), and the life of its citizens is one of moderate and simple bodily satisfaction (372a-c). The city is founded on the division of labor, which is in turn ostensibly rooted in natural distinctions that suit different human beings to different tasks (370a-b). The principle of the division of labor—"one man, one job"—is the basis of justice in the city, which, along with injustice, is to be found in the mutual need that binds its citizens together (371e-372a; cf. 423d).

The division of labor in accordance with nature will also turn out to be the basis of justice in the City of Adeimantus and the Kallipolis as well (cf. 433b). In all of these regimes, however, the relationship between nature, necessity, and justice is highly problematic. Socrates begins from the assumption that it is just to give each the task that best fits his nature. Thus, those with sound minds but weak bodies are fit to be traders, and those with strong bodies but weak minds are best suited to manual labor, but not to full-fledged citizenship (371c-e). Even such general distinctions, however, cannot provide a foundation for political order unless humans are predisposed to do what is just in the above sense. The first city is unreal or mythical insofar as this is not a political problem: as in a beehive, nature has supposedly provided each member of the community with a disposition to do just that task for which nature has fitted him. What is more, in the first city nature seems miraculously to furnish as many individuals of each kind as are required to perform each necessary task, thus ensuring that the satisfaction of needs coincides with the best and most just distribution of jobs: there is no government in the first city, yet there is also no poverty (such as would result from over- or underemployment) or civil strife (372b-c).

So far, we have seen that Socrates, like Hesiod, mythologizes the role of nature in providing for the satisfaction of human needs. In so doing, Socrates exaggerates the natural foundations of justice in a political community and thereby understates the problem of injustice. Still more important, Socrates' desire to minimize the problem of injustice leads him to suppress the erotic and spirited nature of the human soul in describing the first city.

The first city, Glaucon complains, is "without relishes" (372c), meaning that its inhabitants are vegetarians (cf. 373c). Whereas hunting and meat-eating are connected with spiritedness, war, and the competition for glory (witness the tremendous barbecues in the *Iliad*), the members of the first city are singularly unspirited. There are no competitions of any sort among them; they strive for neither honor nor excellence. Their desires are simple; their appetites for sex, food, and drink are moderate (372b-d); and they are free from *pleonexia* of any sort. As a result, they live in peace among themselves—Socrates does not explain how they avoid conquest by *other* cities, especially since they have no army—but neither seek nor gain such immortality as is won by outstanding deeds and speeches. Their lack of *thumos* signals an absence of psychic tension and thus a general erotic deficiency. Bereft of a sense of incompleteness, they are without intellectual or artistic endeavor. They have no sculpture, painting, poetry, history, or philosophy.

Glaucon aptly calls the first city a "city of pigs" (372d). Although its inhabitants are quite moderate in the satisfaction of their bodily desires, they resemble Odysseus's bestial crew in a deeper sense: they too have "forgotten" (or, rather, never possessed) those characteristically human desires that extend beyond the body. Like animals, they possess *erōs* in the sexual sense but not in any of its broader, distinctively human senses. Nor do they distinguish themselves from the animals by the ritual of sacrifice, which involves eating the cooked flesh of the animal victim. Sacrifice ritualistically reconfirms the cosmic hierarchy of gods/humans/animals: gods and men wield fire, but animals do not; animals and men must eat, while gods are immortal and so need only the fragrant smoke of burnt offerings (Vernant 1987, 108*ff*). The vegetarians of the City of Pigs do, however, "sing of the gods" (372b). Socrates evidently means to suggest that there can be no political community without civic gods and a shared sense of the sacred.

Glaucon, whose character emblematizes the deep connection between *erōs* and *thumos*, urges that this City of Pigs be given relishes and other luxuries "in accordance with *nomos*" (372d). Glaucon's request yields a community that resembles actual cities in its "bulky" profusion of luxuries (372e-73d). Socrates calls this a "feverish city" as opposed to the "genuine" and "healthy" city of necessity (372e). Yet Socrates allows that in considering the Feverish City "we could probably see in what way justice and injustice *naturally grow* in cities" (372e; my italics). Socrates thus admits that feverish behavior springs from human nature, which is to say that the City of Pigs has at best exposed only part of the bedrock of *phusis*. Natural necessity is the beginning of the city in a temporal sense, and it is also a principle of the soul's political activity. But the inhuman character of the City of Pigs teaches that our primordial physical needs are not the only, and certainly not the definitive, beginnings of the city and the human soul.

If the City of Pigs is deficient because of the absence of *erōs* and *thumos*, the Feverish City is characterized by psychic and political illness. The liberation of *erōs* introduces into the city poets, rhapsodes, actors, choral dancers, and other makers of "music" (*mousikē*; 373b). Since *erōs* is characterized by *pleonexia* and connected with fever, a term that suggests irrationality and hallucination, it leads to the political sickness of war (373e).

The problem of *erōs* is especially visible in the seemingly contradictory nature of musical education in the City of Adeimantus. *Mousikē* comprises all of the activities presided over by the Muses—song, poetry, dancing, drama, painting, and sculpture. In ancient Greece music and physical training or "gymnastic" (*gymnastikē*) were the two main components of *paideia* or political education, whereby the polis attempted to fashion the bodies and souls of its citizens so as to best serve the well-being of the community as a whole.[2] Because music presupposes *erōs*, it is neither possible nor politically necessary in the City of Pigs. In the Feverish City, however, music itself is feverish. Thus, although Socrates endorses the general structure of traditional *paideia* (376e), he thoroughly reconstructs its content in founding the City of Adeimantus. Yet his approach to music remains ambiguous. On the one hand, Socrates conceives of music essentially as the training of *erōs* (403c); on the other, we already have reason to believe that human souls are by nature productive of political sickness just insofar as they are erotic. Furthermore, while the desires that make Gyges' ring attractive to human beings are clearly a source of injustice, philosophic *erōs*, which is unbounded by patriotism (cf. 327a), may itself be dangerous to good political order. Not surprisingly, then, Socrates' attempt to purge the Feverish City of sickness involves measures designed broadly to suppress the soul's erotic character.

EMERGING ISSUES: *ERŌS* AND *TECHNĒ*

Socrates' paradoxical treatment of *erōs* ultimately reflects deep tensions within the human soul. Insofar as *erōs* is tyrannical and unjust, it must be subdued by the city; insofar as it is essential to being human, it must be nurtured. Education in the City of Adeimantus is largely a matter of restriction and indoctrination: as we shall see, the citizens are tamed like animals, molded like putty, tuned like musical instruments, cured of disease, and dyed like wool with politically salutary beliefs. Philosophical education is admittedly something completely different, for it is an active and erotic process. Yet perhaps even the potentially philosophic soul must first be tamed, molded, tuned, cured, and dyed if it is to have any hope of pursuing philosophy. If it is not so treated, Socrates leads us to ask, how will it avoid erotic corruption? But if it is, one might retort, how will it ever learn to think for itself? Socrates raises these profound questions in the course of exploring Glaucon's philosophic potential, and he continues to wrestle with them throughout the *Republic*.[3]

A related issue concerns the status of politics as an art. As is suggested by the abundant metaphors of breeding, doctoring, and manufacturing, the City of Adeimantus and the Kallipolis may be viewed as experiments in the *technē* of producing just citizens (cf. 395b-c, where the Guardians are called "craftsmen of freedom"). Our earlier reflections on the nontechnical nature of justice suggest that these experiments will not be particularly promising. A further difficulty is raised by the soul's unfinished, erotic nature and capacity to take on many different looks: if politics is to be a *technē*, must its object not be knowable as a certain kind of being with a fixed and intelligible structure? Socrates' earlier, "alphabetical" image of the soul as a word or set of words—an image to which he returns (402a-d)—provides the requisite structure but does not obviously harmonize with the other images of the soul mentioned earlier.

Socrates' technical metaphors do not ultimately provide a coherent picture of the soul. As we shall see, however, even the inconsistency of these metaphors serves indirectly to illuminate the paradoxical complexity of the human psyche.

8

A Comic Tale of Two Cities

The Feverish City is recognizably human. In purging it Socrates embarks in speech on an extensive odyssey to fantastic lands. Intransigent human reality, however, is never far from sight and frequently obtrudes into Socrates' tale in laughable ways. Indeed, the construction of the City of Adeimantus and the Kallipolis combines humor with brutality in a manner reminiscent of Aristophanean comedy as well as the *Odyssey*. The simultaneously humorous and abominable character of these mythical cities springs essentially from the crude simplicity of their approach to the mysteries of the human soul.

It is in its seriocomic limitations—limitations accessible to the thoughtful reader, if not to Socrates' companions—that Socrates' mythological logos teaches us most about philosophy, politics, and the soul. At the same time, it is in reflecting on the seductive power of the logos over Socrates' companions that we may learn most about the character of Socratic pedagogy.

TAMING GLAUCON: THE CITY OF ADEIMANTUS

Socrates now steers Glaucon toward the question of who is fit to serve in the army and how these Guardians should be educated. Socrates opposes the tradition of the democratic polis in asserting that not all citizens should be responsible for military duty, as dictated by the increasingly important principle of "one man, one job" (374a). He in fact begins to reform the Feverish City merely by the act of naming the Guardians, since their title implies a purely defensive posture.

Because the Guardians are to be drawn from men who resemble Glaucon in their natures, Socrates is implicitly asking Glaucon to consider his own education. Like "noble puppies," the Guardians must have keen senses and be speedy and strong; they must especially have the courage that springs from great *thumos* (375a-b). Glaucon's oath at 375b makes it clear that he appreciates the danger that such men, like wild dogs, will be "savage" to one another and tyrannize over the rest of the citizens, since, as Socrates notes, "a gentle nature is opposed to a spirited one." Spirited dogs, however, can be tamed; insofar as humans resemble dogs, perhaps the combination of gentleness and spiritedness, while not natural, "isn't against nature" (375e).

The City of Adeimantus reflects the moral restraint of its namesake and is therefore suited to the taming of Glaucon's potentially savage or Thrasymachean nature. Unfortunately, to tame Glaucon is not genuinely to educate him. This point emerges clearly in Socrates' use of the dog image. As in the City of Pigs, Socrates obscures the difference between humans and animals when he asserts that men, like dogs, must also be philosophers and lovers of learning if they are to be good Guardians (375e-76c). Dogs, Socrates points out, are angry with unfamiliar people and friendly to those they know. Since a dog "defines what is its own and what is alien by knowledge and ignorance," he asserts, it is a lover of learning (376b). Yet a genuine lover of learning is attracted to—not hostile toward—that of which he is ignorant. Indeed, this is the true mark of philosophic courage. Furthermore, dogs have very limited knowledge, as is evident from their stupidity in being harsh to those who have never harmed them and gentle to those with whom they have never had a good experience (376a).

Socrates emphasizes the close connection between philosophy and *thumos* by mentioning both in the present passage for the first time in the *Republic*. Yet his ironic remark about philosophical dogs is also our first big clue about the chasm separating a genuinely philosophic education from the sort of political education that produces citizens who are willing, as the pre-Socratic philosopher Heracleitus said, "to fight for their *nomos* as if for their city-wall" (Freeman, 27: frag. 44). Despite its revolutionary surface, Socrates' program for educating the Guardians is in the most crucial respect deeply conservative: he endorses the time-honored notion that good citizenship rests on unquestioning reverence for the *patrioi nomoi*, the ancestral customs and traditions peculiar to each city and by which each city distinguishes itself from all others (Rahe, 108-11). This traditional understanding of good citizenship is rooted in emotion, not intellect. It leaves no place for philosophic wonder because it seeks to close off the soul to that which lies beyond the circle of one's own things. Similarly, wonder seems to undercut good citizenship, because it opens one up to that which is foreign and causes one to question the worth of that which is familiar.

Manufacturing Virtue: Music and Gymnastic Like dogs, the Guardians will be trained to feel affection for that to which they are akin. Far from being taught to think critically, the Guardians are inculcated with "correct opinion" (*orthē doxa*: literally, "orthodoxy"; cf. Adam,430c*n*) so as to cultivate appropriate feelings of kinship (cf. 402a, 409b). Since the first and greatest part of this process amounts to the moderation of *thumos*, it is not surprising that the naturally moderate Adeimantus now takes over the discussion (376d). The first portion of education involves music, of which the primary part is false speech. Socrates makes it clear that after being educated in false speech, the Guardians will undergo training in gymnastic (377a: "That's what I meant by saying music must be taken up before gymnastic"). Education in *true* speech is evidently reserved for the philosopher kings of the Kallipolis.

Let us dwell briefly on the latter point. Socrates appropriately begins with a critique of the tales told to young children about gods and heroes, because "the beginning is the most important part of every work. . . . For at that stage, it [a young and tender thing] is most pliable, and each thing assimilates itself to the model whose stamp anyone wishes to give it" (377a-b). Socrates and Adeimantus must therefore supervise the mythmakers to ensure that their tales contain only noble and good models, for what children take into their opinions "has a tendency to become hard to eradicate and unchangeable" (378d). This will result in the elimination of most tales now told (377c-d). The grounds for eliminating these tales is not their falsity but the bad and base nature of their models: Socrates blames above all lies that are "not noble" (*mē kalōs*; 377d). Indeed, Socrates later asserts that "we don't know where the truth about ancient things lies" (382d). Since the ancient things in question are the actions of gods and heroes, Socrates implicitly admits that we do *not* know the truth about the nature of gods and heroes. In the same context, he reiterates that the standard by which the new tales are to be judged is usefulness (382d).

The reforms of Socrates and Adeimantus amount to the substitution of noble lies for base lies. These reforms anticipate the Noble Lie itself, since Socrates notes that the poets will continue to make up similar tales "as they [the children] get older" (378c-d). In fact, Socrates tells Adeimantus a noble lie, since the young man accepts Socrates' claim that the models they are manufacturing constitute the true theology (*theologia*; 379a).

Socrates begins by attacking the poets' depiction of war between divine fathers and sons, for the highly spirited Guardians must be taught above all not to behave angrily or harshly toward their fathers, their fatherland, or their fellow citizens (378b-c). Even if the stories Hesiod told about Zeus's treatment of Cronos were true, Socrates maintains, "best would be to keep quiet, but if there were some necessity to tell, as few as possible ought to hear them as unspeakable secrets, after making a sacrifice, not of a pig but of some great offering that's hard to come by" (378a). This passage alludes to the Eleusinian Mysteries, in which initiates sacrificed a pig (cf. Adam, 378a*n*). Socrates thus anticipates the initiation into the truth of the philosophical rulers of the Kallipolis, who will have to recognize that aggression and conflict are intractable components of human nature, and, more generally, that claims about cosmic order are deeply problematic. Similarly, Socrates asserts that it is "neither holy nor advantageous for us" to say that the gods cause evil: he omits to say that it is false (380c).

Socrates' god or gods—he speaks ambiguously of both one and many, perhaps because multiplicity introduces the possibility of disagreement and strife (cf. *Euthyphro*, 7b*ff*)—are hardly distinguishable from the Ideas. The god never departs "from his own form [*idea*]" and "remains forever simply in his own shape" (380d, 381c). Since the god also lacks nothing in beauty or virtue (381c), it also follows that he is without *erōs* (cf. *Symposium*, 200e*ff*). Socrates and Adeimantus establish as if by legislation—but do not attempt to prove—that god is a cause of all good things and nothing bad (380c). Socrates will later assert that the poets must not sing of the persuasion of gods or kings by bribes (390e; cf. 408b-c). Finally, the god never lies—although this may itself be a Socratic lie—since he has no need for "useful" lies told to enemies or mad or foolish friends: god is fearless, and he is a friend of no one who is foolish or mad (382d-e; cf. 331c).[1]

Socrates has by now purged the poeticoreligious tradition of the unjust and deceitful polytropism that Glaucon praised when he said the ring of Gyges would allow one to act "as an equal to a god among humans" (360c). Having discussed what things must be said to make the Guardians reverent to gods and ancestors and friendly to one another, Socrates goes on in book 3 to speak of the sorts of myths that can encourage fearlessness. His agenda is again guided by the previous conversation: Cephalus embodies just those fears on which poets play.

In discussing the formation of courage, Socrates uses the metaphor of manufacture in a contradictory fashion. While the soul was earlier described as some soft substance to be stamped, its *thumos* is now depicted as iron that must not be overheated by fearful shivering lest it become too soft (387c; cf. 411a-b and Adam, 387c*n*). Furthermore, *thumos* was supposed to be "unmovable" (375a), which would strictly mean that it cannot be stamped; conversely, if it can be stamped, it is not unmovable. In addition, it is not evident whether musical education is equivalent to exercise or medicine—that is, to the production of health or the treatment of illness: Socrates now argues that the rulers may lie insofar as they resemble doctors and the citizens resemble sick men (389b-c). Socrates' subsequent discussion of gymnastic merely deepens this ambiguity: although exercise is meant to maintain health, the account of gymnastic is dominated by reflections on the politically salutary employment of medicine (405c*ff*). Indeed, the word *statesman* (*politikos*) first appears in the *Republic* in describing Asclepius, the founder of medicine, who moderated his art in accordance with the political need for useful citizens (407e). According to Socrates, Asclepius concealed certain cures from his offspring because he knew that it was best for men who could no longer adequately serve the city not to be kept alive (406b-c). Medicine and judging are thus coordinated aspects of the political care of bodies and souls: while the judge cures sick souls and kills the incurable, the doctor does the same with regard to the body, and both act with an eye toward the proper work of the citizen (409e-410a; cf. *Gorgias*, 464b-66a).

Socrates is at any rate now concerned with avoiding what amounts to a sickness of the soul: excessive attachment to one's body and possessions, and the excessive fear that is its corollary. While Cephalus lived as a slave to his body, the decent man will fear slavery more than death (387b). Because he is self-sufficient, he will not be overly distressed by the loss of a relative or of money (387e). Furthermore, his attachment to his body will be slight, since he will be moderate with regard to the pleasures of eating, drinking, and sex (389d-e).

Socrates emphasizes unremitting self-possession in the present context. Self-possession, in turn, is connected with moderation or self-control (*sōphrosunē*) as well as courage. To produce decent men, those kinds of poetry that depict death as something fearful in itself, show gods or heroes indulging in or praising the aforementioned pleasures, or represent them as being overcome by laughter—which is akin to having one's *thumos* softened by fearful shivering—must be banned. The genre of comedy is evidently proscribed, although scornful, self-controlled laughter is acceptable (388d-89a).

The relationship between moderation and courage, however, is problematic. It is clear that moderation is different in the rulers and the ruled: Socrates states that "for the multitude" moderation involves being obedient to rulers (389d-e). More important, moderation seems to be at odds with *thumos*, the seat of courage. The most great-spirited men, such as Achilles, Ajax, and Alcibiades, are given to seemingly mad outbursts of passion and are little inclined to obey even the gods, let alone other men. Such men are especially prone to hubris, the vice of insolent arrogance. These points are brought home by the fact that Socrates repeatedly criticizes Achilles for his excessive attachment to Patroclus and for his insolence to gods and rulers (388a, 390a, 390e-91c), while he calls Odysseus (without identifying him by name) "the wisest of men" and praises him for his endurance (390a, d). Odysseus, it should be observed, was self-controlled but cowardly in open battle; furthermore, Achilles was a truth-teller while Odysseus was a clever liar, a desirable quality only among the rulers.[2] Socrates seeks somehow to combine the characters of Odysseus and Achilles in the ruled, who must be brave but not hubristic, self-controlled but truthful. These qualities of soul may well be incompatible. The example of the dog is of no help, since one would nowhere expect to find a highly spirited animal that is moderate in matters of food and sex.

The theme of self-possession also plays a crucial role in Socrates' account of style (392c-98b) and harmonic modes (398c-403c). Socrates first distinguishes between simple narrative without imitation (*mimēsis*) and imitative narrative, in which the poet conceals himself by speaking "as though someone other than he were speaking" (393a). Imitative poetry is dangerous because the soul is inclined to "get a taste for the being from its imitation," so that even the things it vicariously experiences through poetry, and in this extended sense "imitates," would tend to "become established as habits and nature in body and sounds and in thought" (395d; cf. 605d). The correct style in talking about "mad and worthless men and women"—and, indeed, about most human beings, as Socrates indicates—is therefore simple narrative, which describes bad souls while avoiding the passionate involvement characteristic of imitation (396a, e). Real gentlemen will use imitation only when speaking of good men (396c-d). Hence virtually all of the traditional poets and actors will be banned; Adeimantus austerely states that only "the unmixed imitator of the decent" will be allowed in the city (397d).

Just as courage conflicts with moderation, the political inculcation of self-possession is at odds with the formation of philosophic souls. Socrates suggests that in excluding the other poets, the city closes itself off to a divine kind of wisdom: he asserts that the man "who is able by wisdom [*sophia*] to become every sort of thing and to imitate all things" should first be honored as someone "sacred, wonderful, and pleasing" and crowned like a god before being sent away (398a-b; cf. Adam, 398a*n*). This remark is perhaps not surprising in light of Socrates' own narrative style and that of Plato. In narrating the *Republic* Socrates uses the mixed style of epic, in which a great deal of imitation is combined with a small amount of simple narrative. It can also be argued that, with the possible exception of Adeimantus, none of the men Socrates imitates, including himself, are "decent" in the sense understood by Adeimantus: while Socrates is polytropic, Glaucon, Thrasymachus, and Cephalus are in various ways spokesmen for erotic madness and injustice. Furthermore, Plato is a purely imitative poet, and the Platonic dialogue is "a mixture of all extant styles and forms [that] hovers midway between narrative, lyric, and drama, between prose and poetry" (Nietzsche 1967, 90). Neither Plato, as the author of the *Republic*, nor Socrates, as its narrator, would be allowed within the City of Adeimantus. What other means remain to awaken and nourish philosophic *erōs*?

The arousal of *erōs* is the central theme of Socrates' discussion of harmonic modes, instruments, and rhythm. Glaucon now takes Adeimantus's place in the discussion (398c), perhaps because the present topic is more closely connected with erotic passion than the earlier ones. A harmonic mode is "a combination of features which together denoted a certain type of musical discourse: not only a particular disposition of the intervals but also a specific pitch, modulation, color, intensity, and timbre, all the elements which distinguish the musical output of a particular geographical and cultural environment."[3] Socrates insists on the regulation of harmonic modes and rhythms because he recognizes that these things "most of all insinuate themselves into the inmost part of the soul" (401d). Music is "sovereign" because it shapes the *erōs* of a young soul by training it to take pleasure in certain things and to hate others, and pleasure is our first and most powerful teacher. Good music can therefore train one to "blame and hate the ugly and base" before the age of reason, and so to delight in logos when one matures (402a).[4]

The upshot of Socrates' discussion of these matters is that the city should tolerate only those modes and rhythms that accord with the virtues of the good Guardian, together with the simple instruments appropriate to this music. The soul itself may be viewed as a simple musical instrument with two functions, war and peace. The "violent" work of war calls for courage, while the "voluntary" work of peace calls for moderation. Socrates therefore asks for two simple modes, one appropriate to the production of courage and one to moderation (399a-c).

Socrates develops his suggestion that the soul is a kind of musical instrument in his discussion of gymnastic. Gymnastic is partly concerned with the bodies of the Guardians as instruments for the sake of war that must not be "too highly tuned." In this context Socrates reiterates that the Guardians must resemble hunting dogs (404a-b). The best gymnastic, like the best music, will be "simple and decent" (404b). It turns out, however, that gymnastic exists more for the sake of the soul than the body (410c). Socrates now says that the souls of the Guardians must combine two natures—one spirited (*thumoeides*) and one philosophical (*philosophon*). These two elements of the soul are conceived as strings that must be "harmonized with one another by being tuned to the proper degree of tension and relaxation" (411e-12a). Earlier, Socrates suggested that two different kinds of music—one warlike and one peaceful—tightened and slackened spiritedness alone. He now implies that both music and gymnastic are involved in "tuning" both the philosophic and spirited parts of the soul. Music without gymnastic softens "iron" spiritedness, while without music the part of the soul that loves learning is never "awakened" or strengthened, so that one lives ignorantly and "with force and savageness, like a wild beast" (411a-d).

By doubling the elements of the soul that are to be reared by music and gymnastic, Socrates implies that both the spirited and the philosophic parts of the soul must be appropriately courageous and moderate in times of war and peace. This account, however, hardly justifies Socrates' introduction of a philosophic part of the soul, whose proper activity must be learning, not simply being brave and orderly. Furthermore, by dividing the soul into two parts Socrates merely multiplies the problem of how courage and moderation are to be combined in the Guardians. Finally, Socrates' image of the soul as a two-stringed instrument is curiously limited. If anything, the soul is somehow simultaneously musical instrument, musician, and music.

Music is in itself a promising image of the soul because it is fluid and changing, and in this sense "alive." By representing the soul as a musical instrument alone, Socrates abstracts from its active and erotic character: one imagines that the Guardians lie about like rudimentary lyres, waiting to be plucked and strummed by their owners.

The latter image is of course misleading, even as a description of the City of Adeimantus. While Socrates states that Glaucon has participated in purging the Feverish City (399e; cf. 404d-e), this purge has hardly touched *erōs* and *thumos*, the root causes of "fever." With regard to *thumos*, it is perhaps sufficient to note that the Guardians remain meat-eaters (404b-c). As for *erōs*, Socrates explicitly introduces this topic at 402d, when he states that the noblest and most beautiful thing is also "most lovable [*erasmiōtaton*]." Glaucon, who is familiar with the "mad" and intense pleasures of sex (403a), immediately brings up the topic of his boy beloved.[5] Socrates maintains in response that erotic desire should be "moderate and musical," and have nothing to do with mad pleasures. Yet the law he proposes regarding homoerotic relationships is implicitly an admission that the city cannot control sexual contact. "A lover may kiss, be with, and touch his boy as though he were a son, for fair purposes, if he persuades him," Socrates states, glossing over the fact that fathers kiss and touch their sons in a non-sexual way that does not require initial persuasion. Furthermore, Socrates explains, "[the lover's] intercourse with the one for whom he cares will be such that their relationship will never *be reputed* to go further than this" (403b; my italics). A cynic might argue that this legislation teaches hypocrisy—the widespread vice that Adeimantus most opposes.

Socrates' conclusion that "musical matters should end in erotic matters" (403c) merely opens up further questions. If music cannot restrain sexual desire, can it restrain philosophic *erōs*? If the life of philosophy is the most pleasurable existence, as Socrates argues in book 9 (581d-e), is philosophy immoderate? Or is moderation for the philosopher, like the moderation of rulers, something different from the moderation of the ruled?

We may conclude our discussion of the Guardians' education by noting that Socrates and his companions, acting not as poets but as "founders of a city" (378e-79a), have "rationalized" poetry and thus redefined what it is to be a poet. Genuine poets do not consult models when making their poems; this is Socrates' major criticism of them. Furthermore, Socrates insists that the poets should fashion the style of speech and the musical modes and rhythms to suit the speech itself, and not, as is common practice, the other way around (398d, 399e-400a). In brief, Socrates reverses the poetic process by making logos primary and prior to musical inspiration and emotion. Socrates himself understands well the true origin of poetry: "For a poet is a light and winged and holy thing, and not able to make until he should be inspired and out of his mind, and intellect [*nous*] should no longer be in him" (*Ion*, 534b).[6] In the same dialogue, however, Socrates stresses that inspiration is the source of poetry's mysterious, "magnetic" power over human souls (*Ion*, 533d*ff*). Will the uninspired (because intellectually controlled) poetry of the City of Adeimantus be less powerful, and therefore less effective in shaping men's souls, than poems born from the spirit of music?

Socrates' Serious Doubts: The Noble Lie

Socrates and Glaucon turn next to the topic of who should rule. Like good instruments that can hold a tune, the rulers must always be "entirely eager to do what they believe to be advantageous to the city" (412d-e). Socrates nowhere says that the rulers must possess the intelligent judgment (*phronēsis*) that would guarantee the adequacy of their political beliefs. In fact, the key virtue of the rulers is the opposite of flexible, philosophical judgment: they must be capable of dogged endurance in preserving in themselves the conviction (*dogma*) that one must do what is best for the city (412e; cf. 413c, 414b). Potential rulers must be tested by being cast into terrors and pleasures—the Circean bewitchers of the soul that most of all cause forgetfulness (412e, 413b-e)—like colts among noise and confusion or gold in fire (413d-e). Socrates later identifies as courage just this power to preserve "right and lawful opinion [*doxēs orthēs te kai nomimou*]," much as good, white wool that has been well dyed keeps its color under all conditions (429d-30b).

Those who pass the test will be called "complete Guardians," appointed as rulers, and given honors and prizes (as in the Cave); the younger Guardians will be their Auxiliaries (414a-b). But there is a hitch, arising from the fact that men care most for that which they love, and love most that which they identify as their own (412d). The Guardians will need help in persuading the Auxiliaries and the rest of the citizens (if not themselves) to regard the city as their own, so as to prevent them from even "wish[ing] to do harm" to it (414b-d).

It is at this point that Socrates very hesitantly introduces a medicinal, "noble" lie of the sort one tells mad or foolish friends. His hesitancy arises in part from the preposterousness of the lie, which may at best persuade the descendants of the city's inhabitants if it is told as a tale about the original citizens (415c-d), and in part from the fact that he is impiously usurping the role of the oracle of Apollo at Delphi, whose special province is "the founding of temples, sacrifices, and whatever else belongs to the care of gods," including cities, as Socrates implies later in the same passage (427b-c).

All political communities have legends relating to their origins. As a foundation myth within the larger myth of the City of Adeimantus, the Noble Lie is emblematic of Socrates' critical reformulation of the poetic tradition. It combines the myth of authochthony common to many Greek cities, including Athens and Thebes (see Euripides, *Ion*, 20, 30; *Bacchae*, 1314-15), with the Hesiodic tale of the ages of man distinguished by different metals (*Works and Days*, 106-201). The citizens will be told that their education was a dream, and that they were actually molded and reared within the earth. They must therefore defend the earth as their mother and their fellow citizens as their brothers (414e). In addition, the citizens have different metals mixed into their souls at birth by the god who fabricated them: gold for the Guardians, silver for the Auxiliaries, and iron and bronze in the farmers and other craftsmen. The Guardians must above all keep watch over the metals in the souls of the citizens, believing an oracle that the city will be destroyed when an iron- or bronze-souled man becomes its ruler (415a-c).

The Noble Lie's representation of natural providence is comparable to that of the quasi-Hesiodic myth of the City of Pigs: nature (or the god) fashions and marks a variety of men to suit the variety of political jobs. Citizens are natural resources, and the Guardians are miners of men. Socrates does not mention that it will be impossible for anyone but the Guardians to perceive the metal of souls, nor does he speak of the problem this raises about how the Guardians will persuade the rest of the city to accept their rule and authority regarding the proper employment of citizens. The religious authority of the Lie is Socrates' response to these difficulties: the Lie indicates that the Guardians should be obeyed because this course alone is sanctioned by the gods.

The Noble Lie also anticipates the stronger, nonmythical measures whereby the Kallipolis will attempt to guarantee that all citizens regard one another with the *philia* appropriate to blood relations. That stronger measures will be necessary is already evident. Socrates alludes to the Phoenician hero Cadmus, the legendary founder of Thebes, when he introduces the Noble Lie as "a Phoenician thing" (414c; cf. Adam, 414*cn*). The Lie is precisely the kind of ennobling falsehood Cadmus recommends in Euripides' *Bacchae*; when Pentheus, Cadmus's grandson, refuses to accept the divinity of his cousin Dionysus, Cadmus tells him, "Even if this [Dionysus] is no god . . . let it be said by you that he is. Lie nobly . . . in order that it may confer honor on our whole family" (333-36). More important is the story of Cadmus himself. Cadmus populated Thebes with men who sprang up from the planted teeth of a dragon he had slain. These sown men unfortunately sprang forth from the ground heavily armed and immediately began to kill one another.[7] Having himself attempted to charm and then to slay the Thrasymachean serpent of injustice (cf. 358b), Socrates is clearly concerned with the possibility of poisonous, Cadmean fratricide in his own city "when we have armed these earth-born men" (415d). The greatest danger stems from the Auxiliaries, who may turn from sheep dogs into wolves and destroy the flock they are supposed to guard (416a; cf. 415d-e, 422d).

The strongest safeguard against such bestial savagery is a good education. Glaucon, who has by now grown attached to the city he has helped to fashion, insists that the Auxiliaries have been provided with just such an education, but Socrates is doubtful (416b). He therefore recommends additional measures so as not to "rouse up" the Auxiliaries "to do harm to the other citizens," including restrictions against the possession of private property, houses, and money (416c-17b). It is worth noting that if the possession of these things can make the Auxiliaries enemies of the other citizens, "hating and being hated, plotting and being plotted against" (417b), the iron- and bronze-souled citizens, on whom Socrates places no such restrictions, *are* presumably enemies of one another.

Defending the City: Socrates' Comic Apology   At the start of book 4 Socrates is charged by Adeimantus with the task of defending the logos against the accusation that the Auxiliaries are unhappy (419a-20b). Socrates rests his case on the claim that the entire city was to be made happy, not just one part of it, and that in any event he and his companions constructed the city in order to illuminate the nature of justice (420b-c). Socrates goes on in book 4 to complete the City of Adeimantus and then to examine it as a model of justice.

Adeimantus's word *apology* (419a, 420b) implies that Socrates' exposition is somehow a defense of philosophy, particularly against the charge of impiety. How so? I propose that book 4 defends philosophy indirectly and comically, by repeatedly calling attention to the laughable failure of the City of Adeimantus either to sustain itself as a unity or to clarify the nature of the virtues. The Noble Lie is impious by conventional standards, but Socrates deflects (or at least postpones) the charge of impiety to the extent that he ironically dissociates himself from the city. In addition, the outlines of the truly philosophic nature are partly visible beneath Socrates' speech, as in a palimpsest.

Socrates tells Adeimantus at 427c-d that his city has been founded. The place is evidently quite dark, for the next step, Socrates says, is to "get yourself an adequate light" so that justice can be found (427d). Glaucon interrupts at this point, insisting that Socrates must help. It now seems that there is enough light for good visibility after all: Socrates goes on to say that the city is "plainly" wise, courageous, moderate, and just—"plainly," Glaucon responds—and that if the first three virtues can be located in it, justice will "plainly" be whatever is left over (427e-28a).

Socrates soon points out the absurdity of these claims. The group locates wisdom (*sophia*) in the "good counsel" and "craft of guarding" of the Guardians (428b, d)—"I don't know how," Socrates admits (429a). His wonder is well-founded, since the education of the

Guardians focused only on producing courage and moderation. The difference between these virtues and wisdom is great: Socrates next explains that courage is the preservation through everything of opinion formed by *nomos* and dyed into one's soul (429a-30c). His remark that this saving endurance is merely *political* courage, and that the topic of courage can be gone through "still more nobly and beautifully [*kallion*]" (430c), alludes to his own antinomian, philosophical courage and thereby emphasizes the tension between political *paideia* and philosophical education. It is worth noting, however, that the philosopher is also courageous in the conventional sense: life and death do not seem great to one whose desires are focused on "all time and all being" (486a-b).

Glaucon now shows once again that Socrates' mythological logos has pedagogical benefits: when Socrates asks if they can skip moderation—the Adeimantean virtue Glaucon most needs—and go right to justice, the youth strongly objects (430d). Moderation, it turns out, is unanimity about who or what should rule—specifically, "calculation [*logismos*] accompanied by intelligence [*nous*] and right opinion [*orthē doxa*]"—in the city as well as within the soul of each citizen (431c). Unlike courage and wisdom, moderation does not reside in a single part of the city but is a "harmony" that "stretches throughout the whole" and makes all parts of the city "sing the same chant together" (431e-32a). Since only the Auxiliaries and the Guardians have undergone training in moderation, however, we may doubt Socrates' claim that there is "an accord of worse and better" (432a) within the souls of all of the citizens. Indeed, the Noble Lie is necessary largely because of this disparity in education, which is in turn rooted in a disparity in natural capacities. Furthermore, we have already seen that moderation is different in the rulers and the ruled—not to mention philosophers, whose very *erōs* for wisdom, Socrates later explains, makes them moderate in other respects (485d-e). It is therefore misleading to suggest, as Socrates does, that moderation is a harmony, for *harmonia* does not imply polyphony of any sort: Greek choruses before the fourth century B.C. sang either in unison or at octave intervals (Comotti, 12).

Socrates emphasizes the darkness of the City of Adeimantus more than ever now that we have come to the topic of justice. If justice is really in danger of "disappear[ing] into obscurity" unless we trap it like hunters tracking quarry at night (432b), it must not be an abiding possession of the community. Alternatively, there may be nothing remaining beyond the wisdom, courage, and moderation that have already been discovered. As in a cave, the footing is bad (*dusbatos*) and the place is "steeped in shadows" (432c; cf. 434e-35a, where Socrates speaks of kindling a fire in order to see). In case the intrinsic absurdity of the argument is not yet evident, Socrates states that he and his companions are "most ridiculous" since they did not notice that justice is "rolling around" at their feet (432d; cf. 479d). Justice, he asserts, is "the practice of minding one's own business" (433b), whereby each part of the city performs its appropriate task.

There are at least two problems with this definition. First, it is not at all clear that anything was left over from the previous inquiry. How does "minding one's own business" differ from the other virtues taken together—the wisdom by which the Guardians rule, the courage by which the Auxiliaries guard, and especially the moderation by which the city as a whole agrees about what each part is to do? Second, minding one's own business involves not "being a busybody [*polupragmonein*; literally, "doing many things"]" (433d). The Guardians, however, regulate virtually all aspects of the lives of the Auxiliaries and most aspects of the life of the community as a whole; they have absolute power to invade the traditionally private sphere of the family (cf. 421e-22a, 423b-d). Is it not therefore ridiculous to maintain that the Guardians mind their own business?

Socrates' construction and defense of the City of Adeimantus underscores the complexity of the soul and the tension between philosophy and politics. Socrates now admits that the present method of inquiry is not adequate to the precise understanding of the soul but that "another longer and further road" is needed (435c-d; cf. 504a*ff*, where the "longer road" is identified with the study of the Good). After applying the image of the city to the soul, Socrates tells Glaucon that "that dream of ours"—namely, that the city would provide a model of justice—"has reached its perfect fulfillment" (443b). These words echo the *Odyssey* at 19.547, where Odysseus's wife, Penelope, relates her dream that her husband has come home. In a larger sense, the dream to which

Socrates refers is the dream of philosophic homecoming. That this dream is far from fulfillment is evident from Socrates' remarkably weak conclusion that "if we should maintain that we have discovered the just man and city, and what justice really happens to be in them, I think we would not seem to be lying to a very great extent" (444a).

In her dream Penelope is told that she is in fact experiencing "a waking vision of good" (*Odyssey*, 19.547). In constructing their cities Glaucon and Adeimantus are also like men who dream they are awake. Only Socrates is fully "awake" in that he knows these cities are merely the luminous dreams of slumbering men who imagine that they have left the cave (cf. 520c, 534c-d).

TAKING TO THE SEA: THE JOURNEY TO KALLIPOLIS

Having said that Plato's brothers are dreamers, we must nonetheless acknowledge Socrates' educational accomplishment: by means of his philosophical mythmaking he has succeeded, temporarily if not permanently, in making Glaucon a defender of moderation and turning the desires of his companions toward philosophy. The distance between the actual and mythical communities formed in the *Republic* is never greater than at the outset of book 5. Socrates intends at the beginning of book 5 to go on to discuss the decay of the just regime, but his plan is once again foiled. When Polemarchus and Adeimantus "arrest" Socrates for robbing them of the section of the argument pertaining to women and the generation and rearing of children, they reenact the detention of Socrates in the Piraeus at the outset of the dialogue (cf. esp. 327b with 449a-b). The language of the political assembly—voting and passing resolutions—reappears in this context as well (449d-50a; cf. 328b). Yet while in book 1 Socrates was constrained by a mixture of force and persuasion to yield to the nonphilosophic desires of the many, the present community is distinctly philosophic: Socrates' companions, including Thrasymachus, now detain him for the explicit purpose of continuing to listen to philosophic logos (450b; cf. 472a-b). The fact that their desire to learn is mixed with sexual interest in no way diminishes Socrates' accomplishment in awakening their philosophic *erōs*. To the contrary: it highlights the antiphilosophical violence and inhuman absurdity of the restrictions on *erōs* that Socrates is about to introduce.

The peak of philosophic interest among Socrates' companions occurs at a decidedly low point of the argument, which also happens to be the high point of its impiety. Socrates is now more hesitant than ever to continue because what follows will be still more doubtful than the preceding discussion, particularly in regard to its possibility and goodness (450c-d). Socrates' doubts are reinforced by his imagery: while at the end of book 4 he claimed (ironically) that the logos had reached a lookout point, he now says that he must climb up along a slippery path, as if ascending from a cave (445c, 450d-51a). This attempted ascent also involves a great risk of impiety: Socrates anticipates that the argument will make him "an unwilling murderer"—an act that involves religious pollution (451a; cf. *Euthyphro*, 4b-c). He later explains more specifically that he "shrank from touching the law concerning the possession and rearing of children" (453c-d)—the second of the three waves of paradox he endures in book 5, which asserts that men will hold all women and children in common. (The first wave, which begins at 451d and is named at 457b, asserts that male and female Guardians must share all pursuits in common. The second wave is introduced at 457c-d, and the third wave, that philosophers must be kings or kings must become philosophers, is first mentioned at 472a and introduced at 473c-e.)

Socrates' remark that he is prostrating himself before Adrasteia (451a)—an allusion to Aeschylus's *Prometheus* ("The wise prostrate themselves before Adrasteia" [936])—helps to explain his fears. The goddess Adrasteia, who is identified in Greek mythology with inescapable Nemesis, the distributor of divine retribution, punishes acts of hubris against the gods and sacred laws. Since the second wave violates the sacred prohibition against incest (461e), Socrates has good reason to fear Adrasteia: the construction of the Kallipolis involves a hubristic assault on both the ancestral traditions of the polis and the realm of divine law.

This is not all. Plato elsewhere identifies Adrasteia with divine necessity or *anangkē*, which Adam suggests this goddess may originally have personified (*Phaedrus*, 248c; Adam, 451a*n*). Necessity is precisely what Socrates, with Promethean arrogance, attempts to overcome in the Kallipolis. In discussing the second wave, Glaucon speaks of the difference between geometrical *anangkē* and erotic *anangkē* (458d). Glaucon's remark is quite precise, since the regulations pertaining to sexual intercourse constitute an attempt to subordinate erotic necessity to the calculative *technē* of eugenics (cf. 460a). As the Nuptial Number makes clear, this attempt fails: the city ultimately bows to the ineluctable power of *erōs* (546a-47a).[8] Socrates' remark about Adrasteia anticipates this failure, but it also suggests that the attempt to conquer *erotic* necessity involves a crime against things sacred and divine. Socrates' fear of religious pollution becomes fully intelligible if we understand Adrasteia as the divine personification of erotic necessity in particular. Viewed in this light, erotic necessity is *itself* somehow divine, so that the Kallipolis's systematic debasement of human *erōs* is an assault on something sacred and godlike in us.

The striking contrast between the eroticism of Socrates' companions and the erotic restrictions introduced in book 5 suggests that Socrates' gravest impiety in founding the Kallipolis consists in doing violence to philosophy itself. As we shall see, his account of philosophic education in the images of the Sun, Line, and Cave establishes the daimonic or semi-divine and intermediate character of philosophic *erōs* for which he argues in the *Symposium* (201c*ff*). In the present context, Socrates' defense against the charge of impiety consists once again in his comic detachment from the city. As in the case of the City of Adeimantus, however, Socrates' attitude toward the Kallipolis— which resembles the former, except for the three waves of book 5 and the education of the philosopher-kings—is complex. It has recently been plausibly argued that Socrates is serious about the possibility and goodness of the first wave, but not of the second and third waves.[9] Here we shall focus on the last two waves, paying special attention to the Aristophanean components of Socrates' presentation.

The Second Wave: Brutalizing *Erōs* Book 5 is rich with literary allusions. In leaving a cave, taking to the sea (453d), and being buffeted by three large waves, Socrates and his companions metaphorically reenact Odysseus's voyage from the cave of Calypso to the island of the Phaeacians.[10] Since the word for "wave" (*kuma*) also means "fetus," one could say that we witness in book 5 the birth pangs of the Kallipolis. In addition, Socrates frequently alludes in book 5 to comic drama and the comic themes of Aristophanes—particularly to the *Assemblywomen* and the *Clouds*.[11] In implicitly acknowledging the justice of an Aristophanean criticism of the Kallipolis, Socrates distances himself from the logos. Socrates' comic, ironic detachment from the second wave in particular anticipates his full display of philosophic piety in the remainder of the *Republic*, wherein he completes his response to Aristophanes.

Socrates says that he will now turn to "the female drama" (451c). That he has comedy in mind is clear from his repetition of the word *laughable* (it appears six times in 452a-d); his explicit mention of making comic drama at 452d; and his introduction of the typically comic themes of sexuality and bodily ugliness. Glaucon's shock ("By Zeus!") at the notion of hideous old ladies exercising in the nude (452a-b) calls to mind Aristophanes' *Assemblywomen* (976*ff*), in which one old hag after another demands sex from a young man. The latter situation results from the fact that the women of Athens, having commandeered the Assembly and established that property and women shall be held in common—measures enacted in the Kallipolis as well—have made a law requiring men to have sex with ugly women first. Although Socrates is for now concerned with the claim that females too can be Guardians and should be trained in gymnastic just as men, his remark about nude old women must be connected with his emphasis on the animalic nature of human sexuality. The reason is that ugliness and beauty are erotically relevant to human beings, but not to animals. Similarly, sexual *erōs* in the Kallipolis officially has nothing to do with beauty. It is tolerated only for the purpose of reproduction; from the city's point of view, it would be best if men really could be mined from the earth and thereby produced without sex.[12]

Socrates twice discusses, at some length, the stripping of the female Guardians (452a-d, 457a-b; cf. 473e-74a). The image of stripping is emblematic of what transpires in book 5 as a whole, as well as of Socratic discourse in general (cf. *Theaetetus*, 169a-b). As artificial products that are worn because of shame in the face of convention (cf. 452c) and that closely reflect current fashion, clothes are symbols of *nomos*. The naked body, in contrast, is a symbol of *phusis*. To strip is to expose one's naked body and thus to peel away *nomos* so as to uncover *phusis*. This is precisely what Socrates does in book 5, where he claims to establish laws that are in accordance with, rather than contrary to, nature (456b-c). Notably, Socratic philosophizing is also closely associated with stripping in the *Clouds* (177-79, 497-98, 719, 856-59, 1103, 1498), in which the removal of clothing underscores in particular Socrates' reduction of human beings to animals, who do not wear clothes. Given the Aristophanic atmosphere of book 5, Socrates' use of the metaphor of stripping may be read as an implicit acknowledgment that the conception of *phusis* on which the second wave is based is radically unsuited to human beings. We should also note that Odysseus loses his clothing in the sea while journeying from Ogugia to Scheria, as is appropriate for one who has undergone a transition analogous to birth (cf. Segal 1974, 484).

Having again compared the Guardians to dogs and their young to puppies, Socrates says that the difference between the sexes amounts to this: "the female bears and the male mounts" (454d-e). The Greek terms for "bears" and "mounts" are typically applied to animals. The Guardians are to be bred like cocks and dogs, the two kinds of animals especially connected with Socrates' teaching in the *Clouds* (see esp. 491, 810, 1430-31), and like horses (459a-b). For the purposes of the Kallipolis, it is not enough to show that human sexual *erōs* is fundamentally bestial: Socrates goes on to argue that animal *erōs* is diseased. The symptom of this disease is indiscriminate mating, which is politically irrational in that it disregards the city's need for the best possible citizens. The problem of human breeding is a delicate one, because humans are smarter than animals. By way of treatment, the rulers must courageously use as drugs "a throng of lies and deceptions," including rigged mating lotteries, in order to ensure that the best men and women have intercourse most frequently while the worst have intercourse least often (459d-60a). Offspring from these marriages will be reared in a "pen" such as those in which young animals are kept, and mothers will be brought into these pens like cows for milking (460c-d). Just as we might drown kittens, illegitimate babies and those born of parents beyond the prime age of mating will be destroyed (460c, 461b-c).

Socrates asserts, without argument, that the unity of the city is the greatest political good (462a-b). The main causes of political faction are three: money, children, and relatives (464d-e). Socrates clearly does not trust the power of the Noble Lie to convince citizens that they are all part of a single family. Other means are therefore necessary, including the elimination of the nuclear family and monogamy, the immediate removal of children from their mothers, and devices to ensure that mothers do not recognize their biological children (460c-d). In response to Glaucon's question about how the city will prevent incest between parents and children (cf. *Assemblywomen*, 635-36), Socrates admits the possibility of incest between sisters and brothers (461c-e). He argues, however, that the citizens will be most closely united because everyone will regard every other citizen as a family member. In particular, Socrates asserts that the city is bound together best when a community of pleasure and pain exists, and that such a community—which most resembles "a single human being"—comes into being when only the body remains private, and everything else is held in common (462*aff*).

We have already observed that the geometrical control of *erōs* ultimately proves to be impossible. Whether it is best is, as Socrates indicates (450c), seriously dubitable (cf. Hyland 1990, 97-102). There seems in particular to be a deep irony in Socrates' constant references to the highly sacred character of the sexual unions euphemistically called "marriages" in the Kallipolis (458e, 459e-60a, 461a-b). If human marriage is sacred, it is so because it transcends animal sexuality. Since sexual desire is limited in the Kallipolis to politically necessary copulation, however, it does not transcend itself in any of the usual ways. In particular, it leads neither to a deepening recognition of beauty in the soul of the beloved (cf. *Symposium*, 210*aff*) nor to the initimacy of the family. The second wave's reduction of *erōs* to a narrowly limited corporeal appetite cripples the polis as well as the individual soul, for it is surely within the context of the family that the attachments and virtues appropriate to membership in a larger community are first formed (cf. Bloom 1987, 47-137). Socrates' acknowledgment that the citizens will fight with one another casts doubt on whether these virtues and attachments will ever be developed in the Kallipolis: Pheidippides' violent treatment of his father, Strepsiades, in the *Clouds* is perhaps a more likely outcome.

Philosopher-Gods: The Third Wave

Socrates maintains that the rule of philosopher-kings is the smallest possible change required to transform an existing city into a regime "most closely approximating what has been said" (473a). He also mentions that more than one change may be necessary (473b). Socrates later states that in fashioning the dispositions of the citizens, the philosophic ruler will have to start, as would a painter, by wiping clean like a slate both the city and the souls of human beings—"and that's hardly easy," he observes (501a). The difficulty Socrates has in mind emerges only at the end of his discussion of the Kallipolis, where he delicately explains that the philosophic rulers will "send out to the country" everyone over the age of 10 and rear the remaining children in accordance with the principles of the just city (540d-41a). Socrates neglects to mention the violent opposition the philosophic rulers would no doubt encounter from all those over the age of 10. The brutal tactics of the Khmer Rouge in Cambodia, which during the 1970s liquidated "corrupt" older generations in its quest for communistic justice, represent one way of dealing with such opposition. Perhaps the greatest irony of the just city is that its foundation involves a massive act of injustice.

Not surprisingly, Socrates' attack on *erōs* extends to his discussion of the nature of the philosophic rulers. Like the gods of the just city, these rulers are without *erōs*: they no longer strive for wisdom because they are already wise. Indeed, it is only because they already know the truth about what is noble, just, and good that these human beings—men or women (540c)—can best mold the souls of the citizens (484c-d, 500c-501c, 520c). Echoing Parmenides, Socrates explains that those suited to be philosophic rulers "grasp what is always the same in all respects" and so do not wander about like other humans "among what is many and varies in all ways" (484b; cf. 479c-d and

Freeman, 43: frag. 6). In fact, these wise individuals attempt as much as possible to imitate and make themselves like the Ideas (500c).

It is precisely because the philosophic rulers of the Kallipolis are "portrayed as having achieved an epistemological status elsewhere reserved for the gods" (Hyland 1990, 103) that they make good rulers: were they still "wandering" in search of wisdom like Socrates, they could hardly be said to have the sharpest vision of what is and the clearest paradigms of the virtues in their own souls (484c, 501b; cf. Hyland 1990, 104). But if the philosopher-kings combine the virtue of Queen Arete with the mighty intellect of King Alkinoos, Socrates himself is far closer to the roving, polytropic Odysseus than to the rulers of the godlike Phaeacians. Which of these—Odysseus or Alkinoos— best personifies the philosopher?

ODYSSEAN IRONY AND COMIC DISGUISE

Socrates' irony is nowhere more in evidence than in the construction of the city-in-speech. By speaking ironically, Socrates is doubly provocative: while he continues to draw his companions away from the immoderate and unjust attractions of tyranny and toward the relatively courageous, moderate, and just life of philosophy, he invites his extended audience (including Plato's readers) to reflect on the meaning of the argument's deficiencies. Part of that meaning has emerged in this chapter.

Perhaps most important, Socrates has indirectly responded to Aristophanes' charge that he perverts the sacred character of that which is distinctively human. The Socrates of the *Clouds* is concerned with very large things and very small things, but he has no interest in the human soul. Furthermore, he possesses the skill of arithmetical measurement but lacks the capacity to measure the good—a capacity that Plato identifies with *phronēsis* and describes as nonarithmetical measurement "relative to the mean, the fitting, the opportune, and the needful, and everything settled toward the middle ground and away from the extremes" (*Statesman*, 284e). He is therefore wholly ignorant of the sanctity of human *erōs*. In constructing the Kallipolis, Plato's Socrates treats *erōs* in the manner of his Aristophanean counterpart, but he does so like a man trying on and then discarding ill-fitting, grotesque comic masks. By calling attention to the ugly features of these masks, Socrates does more than to show that he is open to desires and attachments that are not purely intellectual: he helps us to appreciate the mysterious beauty and ambiguity of the human soul. In so doing, he also demonstrates the inhuman absurdity of any technical, political attempt once and for all to "solve" the problem of injustice.

The final mask, that of the divine philosopher, has yet to be removed. In terms of the Odyssean subtext, the removal of this mask coincides with Socrates' homeward return from the fantastic domain of the Kallipolis. This return actually begins during the extended inquiry into the nature of philosophy that covers the remainder of book 5 and the whole of books 6 and 7. In particular, the images of the Sun, Line, and Cave illuminate the "wandering," striving character of Socratic philosophizing. In emphasizing the comprehensive *erōs* and living wholeness of the philosopher, these images repudiate as an ironic caricature of philosophy Socrates' earlier description of the superhuman rulers of the Kallipolis, who, like Aristophanes' basket-borne philosopher, "have no leisure to look down toward the affairs of human beings" (500b-c; cf. *Clouds*, 221, 223).

9

Sun, Line, and Cave: Philosophical Imagination and Prophecy

The Ideas and the Good are the gods of the philosopher. They are Socrates' answer to the poetic interpretation of the divine realm first set forth by Homer and Hesiod. In Socrates' account, they are guide-posts of the soul as it journeys through life, as well as both the begin-ning and the end or aim of the philosophic quest for wisdom. Socrates' discussion of the Ideas and the Good thus confirms the possibility of philosophic education and clarifies its nature. Yet Socrates does not discuss the Good directly; he illustrates its nature in books 6 and 7 by means of the philosophic icons of the Sun (507c-509b), the Line (509c-11e), and the Cave (514a-17a). These "likenesses" or "images" (*eikones*) stand together as distinct yet related perspectives within a single speech about the "greatest study" of the Good (505a).

This chapter treats the latter speech as a whole and investigates in turn each of the three just-mentioned images. Socrates' quasi-poetic use of images to speak about what is *like* the highest objects of philo-sophic vision and the soul's relationship to these objects, rather than direct and presumably more precise speech about the Good, the Ideas, and the soul, raises basic questions about the nature and limits of our access to the Ideas and the Good and about the relationship between philosophy and poetry. These questions, in turn, are addressed in and through the images themselves, which are structured in such a way as to account for their own illuminative power.

Socrates first uses the term *idea* to refer to the "letters" or elements of the soul (369a), and the etymologically related term *eidos* ("form") appears initially in connection with the three kinds or forms of good that human beings may choose to possess (357c). Yet it is not until book 5 that Socrates explains what an Idea is, and not until book 6 that he begins to discuss the Good. Let us begin with Socrates' preliminary remarks.

PHILOSOPHERS, IDEAS, AND THE GOOD

To defend the third wave, Socrates is obliged to distinguish genuine philosophers from their sophistical imitators (cf. 487bff). Like Glaucon, the genuine philosopher is erotic (*erōtikos*: 474d). True philosophers are insatiable learners and "lovers of the spectacle of truth" (475e). The Ideas, in turn, first come into view in connection with the soul of the philosopher: they are the special objects of philosophic *erōs* and philosophic apprehension.

Justice and injustice, courage and cowardice, and every Form, according to Socrates, is itself one, but each of these unities appears to be many through its participation in bodies, actions, and other Forms.[1] The many phenomena generated in this manner are images or likenesses of the original Forms or Ideas that show forth in them (476a-c; cf. 479a). The Ideas, then, are the unitary, unchanging, original "looks" or "forms" of things ("Idea" is derived from the verb *idein*, "to see"), in virtue of which each thing possesses its distinct character. The philosopher—who can distinguish these originals from their images, who can catch sight of both, and who, as a lover of wisdom, delights in both originals and images (cf. 488a)—is "awake" and possesses "knowledge" (*epistēmē*); the person who does not acknowledge that there are original Ideas, and could not in any case follow if someone attempted to lead him to knowledge of them, is a "dreamer," possesses mere "opinion" (*doxa*), and is a lover of opinion as opposed to wisdom (476c-d, 480a).

Socrates goes on to explain that opinion is a fallible power that is "brighter" than ignorance but "darker" than knowledge. The objects of opinion are similarly intermediate: they "wander" about, like the unstable beliefs by which we attempt to grasp them, in between the objects of knowledge (the Ideas that participate fully in being and that remain always the same in all respects) and the "object" of ignorance (not-being, or nothing at all) (477a-79d; cf. 484b). Later Socrates identifies the objects of opinion with the visible objects that come into being and pass away, including natural and manufactured objects and their shadows, reflections, and the like (509e-10a, 533e-34a). These changing, visible, and opinable objects, in turn, are likenesses of the unchanging, invisible, intelligible objects or beings (510a; cf. 507b).

Socrates' distinction between knowledge and opinion also plays a crucial role in his discussion of the Good. Once again, the Good comes into sight not on its own, but in relationship to the striving of the human soul. "When it comes to good things," Socrates notes, "no one is satisfied with what is opined to be so, but each seeks the things that are" (505d). Yet while every soul always aims at and pursues that which is genuinely good for itself, without which nothing else is of any advantage to it, the soul is typically "at a loss" about what this might be and "unable to have a stable trust [*pistis*] such as it has about the rest" (505d-e). The Idea of the Good—in light of which the soul's good may be discerned, and by which all things become useful and beneficial—is thus not only the "greatest study" but also the one most indispensable to the welfare of human beings. In addition, it is the study to which philosophers are inevitably drawn by their love of the spectacle of truth, since the Ideas themselves cannot be adequately known without knowledge of the Good (504a-e; cf. 435d, 506a).

PHILOSOPHICAL IMAGINATION: THE SUN AND THE LINE

Why does Socrates have recourse to images in discussing the Good? His explanation is as follows: he does not possess knowledge of the Good, merely opinion, and whereas he is willing to speak about "what looks like a child of the Good and most similar to it"—he means the sun—"it is out of the range of our present thrust" to attain this opinion (506b-e). Despite this clarification, Socrates' procedure is paradoxical. In particular, it is remarkable that in the central passages of the Platonic corpus concerning the Good, Socrates speaks in a manner that seems to undercut the distinction between philosophers and non-philosophers. Given Socrates' account of the different powers and objects of *doxa* and *epistēmē*, how is it that he has only an *opinion* of the Good—the highest topic of philosophic study and learning?

Still more disturbing is Socrates' resemblance to the poets, whom he criticizes in book 10 for being unknowledgeable imitators "at three removes" from the intelligible beings of which visible things—the very things poets imitate in speech—are themselves images (599a; cf. 597e). At the height of the *Republic*'s philosophic ascent, however, Socrates *himself* appears to be at three removes from that of which he speaks, insofar as he substitutes for his opinion about the Good an image, in speech, of the Good's visible likeness, the sun. Is Socrates an ignorant imitator? What, if anything, makes his poetic images *philosophical*?

To begin to answer these questions, we must turn to Socrates' first two images.

The Sun: Prophecy and Philosophical Hermeneutics

Socrates' account of the relationship between the sun and the Good may be summarized as follows. The sun is "an offspring the Good begot in a proportion [or "analogy": *analogon*] with itself" (508b-c). Just as the sun is the "god," "lord," or "king" of the visible things and the visible place, so too the Good "rules as king over the intelligible [*noēton*] family and place"—literally, the family of things that can be apprehended by *nous* (508a, 509d). Each of these two, the sun and the Good, is an *archē* in its own domain (cf. 510b). In particular, just as the sun's energy is responsible for the coming-to-be, growth, and nourishment of the visible things, the Good is the source of the "being" (*to einai*) and "essence" (*ousia*) of the intelligibles. And just as the sun makes possible clear vision, because it bathes the visible things in light and thereby gives the power of sight to the eye, the Good makes possible "knowledge" (*epistēmē*), "intelligence" (*nous*), and

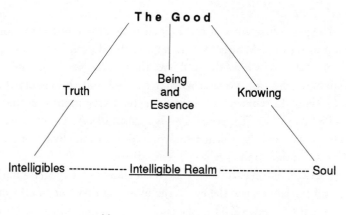

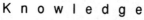

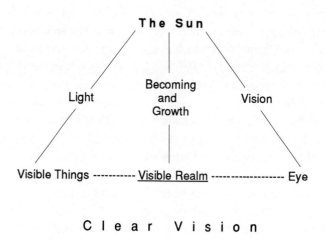

Figure 1. *The Sun* (book 6, 507c-509b)

"recognition" (*gnōsis*) because it contributes truth to the intelligibles and the power of knowing to the soul (Figure 1). As the source of "becoming" (*genēsis*) and growth in the visible realm, the sun is not itself *genēsis*; similarly, as the source of being in the intelligible realm, "the Good isn't *ousia* but is beyond *ousia*, exceeding it in dignity and power" (509b).

The preceding account makes it clear that the Good is the source of the unity of the Whole as a living and intelligible entity: it is the bond or "yoke" that links the soul with the intelligible things, just as its "offspring," the sun, yokes together the eye and the visible things (507e-508a). Furthermore, since Socrates twice mentions that the sun—Helios in Greek mythology—is a god (508a), it is evident that the Good, as a philosophical reinterpretation of our divine origins, is itself to be understood as in some sense divine.

Socrates emphasizes that the Good stands in a special relationship with the soul: since the eye is the most "sunlike" or "sunformed" of the organs of sense (508b), the soul, by analogy, must be especially akin to the Good. To secure for itself what is genuinely good, Socrates indicates, the soul must clearly grasp the nature of its own relationship with the Ideas—especially those Ideas that it may use as models of its own virtue (cf. 504a-e, 484c-d). In this sense the soul "sees" *itself* in the "light" of the Good. Furthermore, insofar as the soul is not fully intelligible apart from "that which every soul pursues and for the sake of which it does everything" (505d-e), knowledge of the Good is necessary for self-knowledge. Yet it is also the case that the soul sees the *Good* in the light of its perceptions of itself: just as being the primary source of illumination and generation on earth is integral to what it means to be the sun, the Good is what it is only in relation to the domain that it lights up, and of which it is an *archē*. This is why Socrates discusses the Good not in itself but in terms of its relationship to the soul and the soul's access to the intelligible things.

These observations begin to explain Socrates' curious allusions at 506b-e to his unspoken "opinion" about the Good. Put succinctly, it would be dogmatic to claim to have anything *more* than an opinion about the Good, because to inquire into either the soul or the Good is to enter into an interpretive or hermeneutical circle in which an adequate understanding of either term presupposes an adequate understanding of the other.

The Sun image gives us one clear reason that the Good must be approached by way of its "reflection" in that which it illuminates: the sustained attempt to observe the Good directly will result in damage to the soul similar to the damage the eye sustains by looking straight into the sun for more than an instant. The damage Socrates seems to have in mind is blindness to, or forgetfulness of, the soul itself (cf. Plato, *Phaedo*, 99d). One loses sight of the Good at the moment when one attempts to dispense with Socrates' procedure of observing it indirectly, in the relationship that it makes possible between the soul and the Ideas. But the soul, like the eye, cannot see itself directly any more than it can see the Good directly. It may observe itself indirectly in its own speeches and deeds, in metaphoric images, or, like an eye looking into its reflection in the pupil of another eye (cf. Plato, *Alcibiades I*, 132cff), in its "reflection" in other souls—that is, in the responses of others to its speeches and deeds. Like the eye, too, the soul cannot critically assess its powers of self-observation without scrutinizing the quality of the light in which it sees—namely, the Good.

The latter observation quite pointedly raises a profound difficulty: What keeps the paradoxical interpretive circle we have been exploring from being a philosophically vicious circle? Without pretending fully to answer this question, we may observe that Socrates speaks of a nonritualistic kind of "divination" as well as "opinion" in connection with both the Good and the soul. In book 6 Socrates uses the verb *manteuesthai* ("to divine") to describe the soul's access in general, and his own access in particular, to the Good: just as the soul "divines that it [the good that it pursues] is something, but is at a loss about it and unable to get a sufficient grasp of just what it is," Socrates "divine[s] that no one will adequately know the just and noble things themselves" before it is known in what way they are good (505e, 506a; cf. 523a). Whether ritualistic or nonritualistic, divination and prophecy are kinds of foreknowledge that lack the clarity, precision, and certainty of, for example, mathematical knowledge.

Glaucon's response to Socrates emphasizes the "prophetic" character of our awareness of the Good: "You divine beautifully" (506a).

Immediately after Socrates' divination, Glaucon asks what the Good is. Since Socrates is unable to persuade Glaucon to drop the question on the ground that Socrates has only an "ugly" and "blind" opinion about the Good (506c), he agrees to leave his opinion aside and speak of the Good in an image. Yet Socrates warns Glaucon not to be deceived by his image, which implies that we are not without resources—presumably intuitive, "prophetic" resources—in judging the adequacy of speech about the Good. Socrates' comment also underscores the sense in which an image so presented—that is, as nothing *more* than a likeness—is nondogmatically open to the possibility of its own fallibility. In this important sense images are especially appropriate to the articulation of philosophic divinations.

A similar passage in book 2 concerns the Ideas and the soul. Socrates bases his decision to found a city-in-speech on an "opinion" that amounts to a divination: his godsend (*hermaion*) that "perhaps" the Idea of justice in the soul will be more visible in the "bigger" letters of the city (368c-69a). Socrates' guarded language and his allusion in this context to Hermes, the messenger god whose communications link the human and divine spheres and who has given the name "hermeneutics" to the art of interpretation, are not inappropriate, for his procedure is circular on its face. In particular, his reason for constructing the city-in-speech is that the soul is too difficult to see on its own (368c-d), but to know in advance that the city resembles the soul one must *already* have made out the soul's looks. Socrates' reference to a gift of Hermes clarifies the logical status of the city/soul analogy: his presupposition about the connection between the city and the soul is not knowledge but a philosophic prophecy that is worth testing.

Broadly defined, philosophic prophecy consists in a certain foreknowledge of the Ideas, the Good, and the soul. It is important to observe that the oracular and prophetic character of self-knowledge and knowledge of the Good is emphasized in other dialogues besides the *Republic*. Most notable in this connection is the *Symposium*, in which Aristophanes remarks that *erōs* is the soul's longing for lost wholeness, and that the soul of one in love "is not able to say, but divines and speaks oracles about what it wants" (*Symposium*, 192c, e). Aristophanes' speech is followed by Socrates' account of his initiation at the hands of a prophetess into the Mysteries of *erōs*, which is itself a *daimōn* (demigod) that interprets (*hermēneuei*) for human beings that which is divine (*Symposium*, 201d*ff*). There is a somewhat comic subtext of religious initiation in Socrates' speech about the Sun as well. When Glaucon suggests that the Good is pleasure, Socrates—the "priest," so to speak, of these philosophic "Mysteries"—reminds him to avoid blasphemy and "use words of good omen" (509a); nevertheless, Glaucon "quite ridiculously" mocks Socrates' final revelation of the Good's extreme dignity and power by exclaiming, "By Apollo, what daimonic hyperbole!" (509c). These remarks prepare us for the further development of the themes of Mystery initiation and prophecy in the Cave image.

Let us now briefly consider what the Line can teach us about philosophic prophecy's dependence on the fundamental role played by imaging relationships within the structure of human experience.

"Seeing Double": Eikasia and the Divided Line   The image of the Line correlates the degree of "truth" of the things in the realm of being and becoming with the relative "clarity" and "obscurity" of the "states" or "affections" of the soul that arise in relation to these objects. The Line (depicted in Figure 2) thus incorporates the main elements of the Sun into another image of the Whole. The top section of the line (BC) accordingly represents both the beings of the intelligible realm and the soul's "insight" (*noēsis*) in relation to these intelligible beings, while the lower section of the line (CA) represents both the visible things in the realm of becoming and the soul's state of "opinion" in relation to these things (509d-e; cf. 534a). Despite its divisions, the Line represents the integrity of the Whole perhaps still more forcefully than the analogy of the Sun: the intelligible and visible domains are now depicted as parts of *one and the same line*. The Line also emphasizes the close connection between the states of the soul and the character of its objects, for the same line is equally a likeness of both.

The Line represents the Whole in two dimensions: the vertical axis is constituted by the relationship between the intelligible and the visible things, while the soul stands in relation to its objects along the horizontal axis. We have already remarked on the interrelationship of

Figure 2. *The Divided Line* (book 6, 509c-511e)

these two dimensions within the basic structure of the philosophical journey that unfolds over the course of the *Republic*. It now appears that the continuity or integrity of the Whole itself depends on the imaging relationships that bind together its elements along *both* axes. The Line, for its part, both elucidates and exemplifies "imagination" (*eikasia*), the power of making and recognizing images that enables philosophic education by allowing us to move "vertically" toward the originals. The Cave, in turn, will shed light on the "horizontal" phenomenon of psychic imitation or mimesis, whereby the soul takes on the character of its objects.

The lowest subsection of the line concerns "images" (*eikones*) and "imagination" (*eikasia*). Since the shadows, reflections (*phantasmata*), and the like that are located at section DA of the line are images of the primary visible objects situated at CD (509d-10a), it would seem that the line leaves no room for images that are not likenesses of visible objects. This would mean, however, that there is no place for the icons of the Sun, Line, and Cave, which are images, not of visible objects, but of the Whole, of which visible objects are merely one part. Yet as Jacob Klein makes evident in his discussion of the Line, *eikasia* extends to intelligible objects and is operative in the interpretation of the Line as a whole.[2]

Subsection CD consists of natural and manufactured objects, about which the soul experiences *pistis* or "trust" (510a, 511e). These primary visible objects, in other words, are things in which we naturally place our confidence; they seem stable and trustworthy, and in this sense "real," especially in comparison with the "fantasms" or shadowy images of the visible things that Socrates places in the line's lowest subsection (DA). Indeed, Socrates' designation of the latter images as "fantasms" brings out an important characteristic of *eikasia*: the power to apprehend images involves seeing the image *as* an image and not confusing it with the original of which it is an image (Klein, 114). As Klein notes, *eikasia* allows us to see the original "through" the image; imagination is thus "a kind of 'double seeing' " (Klein, 115).[3]

Just this kind of "double seeing" takes place when the primary visible objects at CD are *themselves* used as images of the intelligible objects at EC, the lower subsection of the intelligible realm, by the soul that is engaged in "reasoning" (*dianoia*). *Dianoia* comes into play when thought-provoking ambiguity intrudes on the superficial intelligibility of the visible world, so that the soul is called on to explain, in terms of "those things themselves that one can see in no other way than with *dianoia*," that which is evident to sense perception (510e; cf. 523a*ff*). Because the turning of the soul from the domain of becoming and toward the domain of being is crucial to the quest for wisdom, Socrates later places great emphasis on the training of *dianoia*, through mathematical studies, in the education of the potential philosopher (521d*ff*; at 511a-b *dianoia* is associated with "geometry and its kindred arts").

Socrates describes the activity of *dianoia* as follows: "a soul, using as images the things that were previously imitated, is compelled to investigate on the basis of hypotheses and makes its way not to a beginning [*archē*] but to an end" (510b). The hypotheses used by *dianoia*, such as "the odd and the even, the figures, [and] three forms of angles," underlie its investigation of the visible world. These hypotheses, however, are themselves treated "as known" and "as though they were clear to all" (510c); they themselves are not investigated by *dianoia* but instead serve as suppositions on the basis of which one may move, by deductive reasoning, to a conclusion.

Dianoia is "thinking" (*noein*) "through" (*dia*)—in the first instance, thinking through, or by means of, hypotheses. But in exercising *dianoia* the soul also thinks through images drawn from the visible realm: geometricians, for example, use three-dimensional models and sketches in their demonstrations, although "they make the arguments for the sake of the square itself and the diagonal itself, not for the sake of the diagonal they draw" (510d). Because these images—unlike the images located in the lowest subsection of the line—are meant to illuminate the literally invisible but intellectually accessible foundations of the visible world, we are dealing with a new kind of *eikasia*, one that "could rightly be called *dianoetic eikasia*" (Klein, 119).

Finally, it is *eikasia* that allows us to understand the relationship between *dianoia* and the intellectual activity represented by the highest subsection of the divided line (BE), where "insight" (*noēsis*) and "the power of dialectic" grasps Ideas or Forms. Dialectic is the activity of sorting according to kinds through speech. In recapitulating the teaching of the Line, Socrates states that *dianoia* stands to *noēsis* (or *epistēmē)* as *eikasia* stands to *pistis* (534a). In other words, *dianoia*, like the fundamental power of *eikasia* located in the lowest subsection of the line, is itself fully intelligible only in relation to a higher cognitive power and higher objects, of which its own objects are but shadowy images (cf. Klein, 124). The "downward" movement of *dianoia* from hypotheses to conclusions, in turn, is a partial imitation of the double movement of dialectical insight whereby the philosopher is finally able to grasp the Idea of the Good in itself (534b-c): dialectical inquiry moves both "up" to the Good and back "down" to the Ideas in seeking the ultimate foundations of the previously unexamined hypotheses on which dianetic investigation rests (511b-c).

The Line itself, as Klein notes, summons the soul's philosophical imagination in a twofold way. Dianoetic *eikasia* comes into play when we examine the mathematical characteristics of a line that has been divided in accordance with Socrates' instructions to Glaucon (cf. Adam, 509d*n*). But the Line is also an image of the Whole, and as such, "the use made of the geometrical model by Socrates is wholly ungeometrical": the Line becomes a springboard or steppingstone "for leading Glaucon—and us—to an understanding of the difference between the intelligible and the visible and of the different levels within each of them" (Klein, 125).

Once again, Plato emphasizes the interconnectedness of all levels of human experience. In particular, the Line suggests that the literal and metaphorical ascent and descent that is imaged in the *Republic* itself imitates the "upward" and "downward" dialectical movement that characterizes the highest philosophical activity. Furthermore, the images of Sun and Line make it clear that the "prophetic" ascent of the soul toward the Ideas and the Good is made possible by the ramification of imaging relationships throughout the entirety of human experience, for these relationships allow us in some sense to see that which we seek "through" that which is already present to us. Indeed, it would be fair to say that *eikasia is* the power of philosophic prophecy.

Logos is by nature imagistic: it images what is *seen.* Poetry is therefore not open to criticism simply because it is the making of images of images. In fact, Socrates—who is himself a literary image (cf. 376d)—regularly uses such "second-generation" images: the peculiar cave of which Socrates speaks, for example, is an image of a real cave, which is in turn an image "of our nature in its education and want of education" (514a; cf. Klein, 125). Yet certain kinds of poetic and non-poetic images remain open to criticism. Some spoken or written images disguise their intrinsic fallibility by pretending to be originals, and some bring the soul to a standstill rather than provoking further reflection on that which is imaged. Finally, some poetic images may be more prophetic—may more adequately reflect the original and divine foundations of human life that the philosopher speaks of as the Ideas and the Good—than others. We can now suggest an answer to an earlier question: the dialogues are *philosophical* poems because they are provocative, prophetic, and call attention to their status as (mere) images.

The Cave, too, has much to say about the difference between prophetic and nonprophetic kinds of speech. Like its sister images, the Cave points beyond itself toward the dialogue as a whole, in which the deed of learning is most fully imaged and enacted.

THE CAVE IMAGE AND THE PROBLEM OF PLACE

By the time Socrates tells Glaucon to "make an image of our nature in its education [*paideia*] and want of education [*apaideusia*]" (514a), it is the middle of the night and the men have long since grown accustomed to seeing one another in firelight. This setting is most appropriate to a story that uses the images of darkness and flickering flames to emphasize our initial distance from the Good. I use the word *story* because the Cave, unlike the Sun and Line, is genuinely a drama in which distinct characters participate. This drama is meant to illuminate both the problematic context of philosophic education and the range of possible responses to this context. The Cave further suggests that the sorts of training that pass for "education" in political communities in general and in a democratic polis in particular—the teaching of the many on the one hand, and of the sophists and the poets on the other—fail to come to grips with the issue of whether and in what ways the familiar domain of political community may properly be situated within the Whole. Let us call this issue the problem of place.

The problem of place is implicit in Socrates' striking comparison of our condition to that of prisoners chained in a cave, and is raised explicitly when Glaucon calls the image and the prisoners "strange" (515a): the Greek *atopon* literally means "out of place" or even "placeless." On the deepest level, Glaucon's remark points toward the initial and ordinary disorientation of human life, particularly to the placelessness of political communities—their blindness to the problem of being "out of place" and to the meaning of being "in place." To anticipate, the Cave indicates that our human, political habitats are always only partially "in place" within the Whole, in that they are located with respect to, but at the same time distant and detached from, the Ideas and the Good. The image depicts the polis as a place of widespread ignorance and folly. Against this dismal backdrop, the Cave introduces two kinds of human beings—the prophetic poet and the philosopher—who attempt to sustain, in relation to the Ideas and the Good, what could be called the locatedness-within-detachment of the human place. In addition, the Cave contrasts these two similarly oriented souls—both of which are open, in different ways, to the original and divine measures of human life—with the closed soul of the sophist. In its depiction of these three types of souls and of our initial condition of *apaideusia,* and in its identification of philosophy with education, the Cave provides a playbill for the larger educational drama that unfolds over the course of the *Republic.*

The Prisoners' Folly   Socrates asks Glaucon to imagine a cave in which men have been chained "from childhood." Above and behind these prisoners is a wall, over which other men (who are themselves concealed by the wall) move puppetlike artifacts and statues of men and animals. Farther up is a fire, beyond which is the cave's opening and the outer world (514a-15a); outside are also human beings and "other things," presumably including animals, as well as shadows and reflections of these things in water (516a).

As with the Sun and Line, basic imaging relationships bind together the cave and the outer world—the two fundamental parts of the Whole in this icon—as well as the various levels of experience within these two domains. Thus the shadows on the cave wall are images of the "puppets," which in turn are images of the things in the outer world as well as of their shadows and reflections. Because the special focus of the Cave, however, is the emergence of the philosopher from the ignorance and folly characteristic of political communities, the visible and intelligible domains of the Sun and Line are now more richly depicted as a dungeonlike cavern and the bright and blooming world above (517b). Furthermore, the Line's emphasis on natural, mathematical relationships now gives way to a primary concern with ethical standards of direct relevance to human life, such as nobility, justice, and goodness.

Aristophanes represented Socrates' Thinketeria as a gloomy, enclosed, lifeless space, as if to confirm Pheidippides' suspicion that philosophy reduces healthy human beings to the condition of half-dead shut-ins (*Clouds*, 102-4, 119-20, 184-86, 1112, 1171). Plato cleverly reverses Aristophanes' implication by using the same symbolism of confinement in darkness to represent the condition of the prisoners, who are entirely unaware of the basic imaging relationships just noted. The prisoners are "like us," Socrates tells Glaucon. The bonds that fasten their heads and legs would prevent them from seeing anything of themselves and one another, or of the wrought items carried along the wall, other than the shadows cast by the fire onto the cave wall beneath them (515a-b). If they could talk to one another, Socrates adds, they would hold the things they see to be "the things that are," or "the beings [*ta onta*]."[4] They would hold the truth to be "nothing other than the shadows of artificial things" (515b-c). The prisoners, in other words, regard the shadows—the only objects with which they are familiar—as though they were Ideas, for truth and being are the fundamental characteristics of the Ideas (508e, 509b).

Immediately after this clarification Socrates speaks of the "folly" (*aphrosunē*) of the prisoners (515c), a term that implies disorientation of character as well as intellect: *aphrosunē* is the privation both of *sōphrosunē* and *phronēsis*. Socrates then describes the compulsion and pain involved in one former prisoner's upward journey, which he calls a "release and healing from bonds and folly" (515c). These remarks suggest that the whole soul initially habituates or *binds* itself to those objects of its perceptual and intellectual vision represented in the Cave image by the shadows. While the philosopher who has emerged from the cave "imitates" the Ideas (500c), the prisoners' souls imitate and are molded by the shadows (cf. 395d). The prisoners' folly thus derives from the inappropriateness of the shadows as intellectual and erotic measures for the human soul.

In virtue of their truth and being, the Ideas are genuine and stable entities by which the soul may take its bearings. Because the Ideas are "always the same in all respects" (479e, cf. 479a), the soul may "fix" or "support" itself on them (508d). In addition, the soul's clear vision of the Ideas enables it to form itself in accordance with them. Socrates speaks of "grasping" and "begetting" in addition to "seeing" in order to suggest, through this sexual metaphor, the transformative dimension of the soul's relation to the Ideas (490b). The philosophic soul's generative intercourse with the Ideas, however, is unconsciously imitated within the cave by the prisoners' degenerate habituation to the shadows, which they mistake for Ideas.

Socrates suggests that the shadows are an image of the public life of political communities. The action displayed in the shadow play evidently consists of humans making use of natural and artificial means ("animals" and "artifacts") to satisfy their desires. Furthermore, Socrates' remark that the play of shadows proceeds in customary or regular ways (516c-d) implies that the activities visible in the shadow play manifest specific customs and ends, such as those that would characterize the everyday life of a political community.

In fine, Socrates' account of the prisoners' folly turns upon the natural human tendency to regard just those ends and standards shown in the shadow spectacle of public life as the best and most authoritative ends and standards, and, in accordance with the natural, "horizontal" phenomenon of psychic mimesis, to model one's desires and dispositions after the widely shared practices of one's community. The Cave suggests that the spectacle of public life by which humans first take their bearings is radically dependent on human work, which gives the shadows their form and movement. Since the prisoners cannot turn their heads toward the wrought items, they are unaware that human work determines the ends and standards by which their desires and dispositions are oriented. They are thus oblivious to the permanent danger of disorientation introduced by the role of human activity in shaping the measures by which they take their bearings, for it is clear that the existence, accuracy, and distinctness of images of the Ideas in the shadow play depends on who makes and manipulates the wrought items.

Subterranean Competition: The Polis as Underworld

Among the prisoners are "honors, praises, and prizes"—the symbols and substance of power—"for the man who is sharpest at making out the things that go by, and most remembers which of them are accustomed to pass before, which after, and which at the same time as others, and who is thereby most able to divine what is going to come" (516c-d). The prisoners' competition involves determining and remembering what they are looking at, and foretelling what is to come. Since the prisoners compete in "making out the things that go by," what they are looking at is, at least initially, not equally evident to all of them. Success in the competition depends on convincing the other prisoners that one's view of what they are looking at is the best view. Socrates makes clear, however, that the challenge facing the prisoners is not simply or even primarily perceptual: success involves setting forth a persuasive *interpretation* of that which is already visible to everyone. Socrates thus indicates at 520c that the competing judgments the prisoners put forth concern the relative worth of the things they see, as, for example, the nobility or baseness of certain ends, the justice or injustice of certain laws, and the goodness or badness of certain practices.

The issues at stake in the prisoners' competition for power are evidently precisely the sort of issues over which men dispute and form factions in actual political communities. The prisoners' interpretation of the shadows, however, is not anchored in an inquiry into the truth. It is instead subordinated to their desires for honors, praises, prizes, and power—desires rooted in the erotic nature of the soul (cf. 580d-81b). In

Socrates' account, these desires, which are nourished and inflected by the competition, constitute the key mechanism by which *nomos* gains authority over the soul. Like the young man among the many Socrates describes at 492b-d, a young man among the prisoners would give himself over to the prevailing manner of praise and blame (and this would hold true in nondemocratic regimes as well as democracies): it is because his youthful and malleable soul is "swept away" by the example of so many others, and especially by his growing love of the pleasures associated with honor and praise, that he would come to reflect in his thoughts, speeches, and deeds the dominant vision of what is noble, just, and good.

After describing the prisoners' competition, Socrates asks Glaucon whether the philosopher would not "be affected as Homer says and want very much 'to be on the soil, a serf to another man, to a portionless man,' and to undergo anything whatsoever rather than to opine those things and live in that way?" (516d). Quoted in this context, the words of the shade of Achilles, spoken to Odysseus in Hades (*Odyssey*, 11.489-91), anticipate Socrates' suggestion at 521c that we are to compare the prisoners in the cave with the dead residents of Hades. The shades in Hades, "witless phantoms of worn-out men" who flit to and fro "like a dream," cannot recognize Odysseus or speak the truth to him without drinking the blood he provides (*Odyssey*, 11.141-54, 222, 390, 476). Similarly, the prisoners know nothing of the world outside the cave and neither understand nor duly recognize the man who is accustomed to seeing in its light. Although the prisoners take themselves to be educated when they become capable of entering the political competition Socrates describes, their condition is one of *aphrosunē*; without *phronēsis* they act and speak as if "in a dream" (520c). Their unstable souls, like the shades in Hades and the shadows that play across the cave wall, are swept here and there as if they were phantom images.

Talkative Porters and Sophists: Hollow Icons, Empty Mysteries

The men who carry the wrought items are divided by Socrates into two groups: "some of the porters utter sounds while others are silent" (515a). We shall examine each of these groups in turn.

Because of the cave's echo, whenever one of the porters should happen to utter a sound, the prisoners would believe that the passing shadow was uttering it (515b). We may note that Socrates' reasoning about the echo must apply in the case of the prisoners as well, who can see nothing of themselves or one another: a prisoner would believe that the utterances of his fellow prisoners have come from the passing shadows. Hence, the prisoners would be unable to distinguish the source of sounds originating from the porters from those originating from fellow prisoners; in both cases it would seem that the sounds come from the shadows. In addition, whenever the prisoners speak they would understand themselves to be talking to the shadows.

While space does not permit an argument, there is good reason to believe that the talkative porters intentionally make use of the acoustics and optics of the cave in such a way as to engage in the prisoners' competition while concealing from the prisoners their own privileged position.[5] In so doing, these porters use the art of the sophist that Socrates describes at 492b-93d. These porters have a special advantage in the competition: they can utter such sounds as will on each occasion make the prisoners most favorably disposed toward the shadows cast by the items they themselves are carrying, and with which the prisoners identify them. And while they are constrained in this work by the need to adhere to the current desires and convictions of the prisoners, their privileged position within the cave allows them gradually and partially to alter the movements and shapes of the shadows to their own advantage.

It is consistent with the Cave image to suppose that a prisoner could ascend to the level of the wrought items and still focus his interest and attention on the shadow play and the competition. Indeed, Socrates indicates that this is precisely what we may expect, at least initially, of one who is dragged up to the firelight: the prisoner who undergoes this experience turns back toward the shadows (515e), and evidently nothing about his encounter with the wrought items or the men who manipulate them prevents him from doing so. The prisoner who is dragged before the wrought items "sees more correctly" and is "somewhat nearer to what is and more turned toward beings" only because it is now evident to him that the shapes of the shadows and

their movements and interactions within the shadow play are produced by human work.

The preliminary stage of philosophical education is wholly nega-
tive in its effect, not to say nihilistic, for it amounts to the recognition
that the seemingly solid and unchanging "truth" that initially guided
and supported one is in fact fashioned by human beings and contingent on human choices. Because this initial recognition is painful and
disorienting (515c), it is no wonder that the prisoners are hostile to the
philosopher who attempts "to release and lead them up" (517a): like a
thief, the philosopher appears to rob *nomos* of its authority. In this
respect, the philosopher resembles the sophist. Indeed, Socrates' public trial and execution provide a fair indication that the many are
unable to distinguish between philosophy and sophistry.

The Cave offers a compelling reason for the popular confusion
of philosophy with sophistry: educationally, sophistry is arrested or
truncated philosophy. The sophist may be represented in the terms of
the Cave image as one who teaches others how to manipulate the
shadows, having himself ascended only to the level of the wrought
items and then returned to the level of the prisoners. The sophist's
horizons are ultimately no broader than those of the prisoners. Since
the sophist neither knows nor seeks anything beyond the wrought
items and the fire, he teaches his students that humans produce the
measures by which they take their bearings but denies that there are
true and appropriate measures for this productive activity itself.

The Cave also suggests that the difference between the philosopher and the sophist (not to mention other nonphilosophers) is at bottom a matter of nature, and especially of erotic nature. Both the
sophist and the philosopher undergo the same initial experience, but
the realization that humans produce the shadows influences the philosophic soul and the soul of the sophist in opposite ways. While the
prisoner who will finally leave the cave must be compelled and
dragged upward, Socrates also says that the upward turning of his soul
occurs "by nature [*phusei*]" (515c). Socrates' meaning is not difficult to
discern: the desire of a potential philosopher *must* incline by nature
toward philosophy, since it is obvious that a soul without philosophic
erōs could never be compelled to philosophize. According to Socrates,

the pain and confusion of first encountering the wrought items and the fire causes one to want to turn back to the shadows. At the same time, however, the intellectual *erōs* of the philosophically inclined soul is inflamed by the problem of the production of human measures. Such a soul experiences its new insight into the contingent, human foundations of *nomos* not only as a loss but more fundamentally as a *provocation*, and this soul is moved courageously to endure further pain and perplexity in its quest for measures or standards of genuine stability and clarity. The labor pains of intellectual rebirth (cf. *Theaetetus*, 151a-b) begin for such a soul when it first recognizes the depth of its own ignorance.

The souls of the sophist and his students, on the other hand, are hardened in their *aphrosunē* by the same disorienting insight. The sophist's solution to the intellectual and emotional instability engendered by this insight is to cling to the produced measures and to return permanently to the relative clarity of the shadows. According to Socrates, the sophist knows "nothing in truth about which of these convictions and desires [of the many] are noble, or base, or good, or evil, or just, or unjust": he merely calls what pleases the many good and what pains them bad; he calls the necessary just and noble, "neither having seen nor being able to show someone else how much the nature of the necessary and the good really differ." Wouldn't such a man, Socrates asks, be "out of place [*atopos*] as an educator?" (493b-c).

The things to which the prisoners are habituated thus continue to exercise an internal compulsion on the sophists and their students, who do not cease to aim at honor and power among the prisoners and so to share in their basic desires and convictions. The sophist's personal predisposition is reflected in his public speech. Like Thrasymachus (336b*ff*), the sophist preaches the worthlessness of philosophy as measured by the current desires and convictions of the many. In terms of the Cave, philosophy blinds one, or causes one to become erotically and intellectually disoriented (517a; cf. *Gorgias*, 484c-86d).

The sophist, however, inverts the true relationship between philosophy and sophistry. This is most readily apparent in the subtext of Mystery initiation that runs throughout the Cave, in counterpoint to its use in the *Clouds*. Philosophical education repeats the essentials of

ritual initiation in a way that enhances rather than debases their meaning: the prisoner who is led up experiences a passage through darkness; new and strange deeds, speeches, and sights; metaphorical
"death," or the loss of one's old, ignorant, conventionally constructed
self at the level of the wrought items; "rebirth" in leaving the cave—
which functions symbolically both as underworld and birth canal—and
coming, as through birth, into the domain of being; and the final,
bright vision of the sun (= the Good) itself.[6] In contrast, the
"Mysteries" of sophistry, which imitate philosophical ascent in a small
and pale way by initiating one into the acoustics and optics of the cave
and culminating in the vision of the fire, are a sham: they are neither
genuinely mysterious nor divine. Most important, they involve neither
intellectual and emotional death nor rebirth: the sophist never sheds
the bonds of *aphrosunē* or becomes anything other than a clever prisoner. Indeed, in denying the very possibility of ascent from the cave,
the sophist proves to be "out of place" not only as an educator but also
as a prophet.

Silent Porters: Poets and Philosophic Craftsmen   The
sophistical manipulations of the talkative porters must take place
against a received cultural "backdrop" of customs, ends, practices, and
the like. I suggest that the silent porters are responsible for the shadow
scenes that constitute this backdrop of accumulated tradition. If this
assumption is correct, the items carried by these porters surely incorporate or reflect works of poetry of the sort that tend to become
embedded in the traditions of political communities, such as the great
myths of Homer and Hesiod.

On the basis of its primary role in the "education" to be found in
existing political communities, its radical influence in shaping men's
characters, its corrupting content, the ignorance of its practitioners,
and its subservience to the opinions and desires of the many, poetry
would seem to be a sister of sophistry and to deserve a place alongside
it in the cave. Strikingly, however, Socrates' criticisms do not seem to
apply to all poets and all poetry. Socrates indicates that Homer in particular is philosophically prophetic, in that he remains at the educational level represented by the wrought items but is nonetheless able to

discern in the shadow play of human life, and to fashion poetic images of, human qualities that are in some sense divine.

Before we consider the evidence concerning Homer, it is important to reiterate a peculiarity of the Cave image: while the mathematical relationships emphasized in the Line exist independently of human activity, the imaging relationships that connect the cave with the world above do not. The human realm is represented in the Cave image as a place apart from, but situated with respect to, the outer world. But were it not for the presence of the outer world within the cave by means of images of the Ideas that are produced and maintained by humans, we humans would be absolutely disconnected from that in respect to which we could become oriented or find our proper place. Indeed, we could not differentiate between orientation and disorientation, so that humanity and nobility would be indistinguishable from inhumanity and baseness. Without access to any images whatsoever of the Ideas, we would be wholly in the dark, and education, or the improvement of vision, would be impossible. The Cave image, however, indicates that the human realm is in place precisely because and to the extent that humans image the Ideas within it. In this sense, human life qua human points beyond itself to that which is divine, although it is not itself wholly or simply divine.

Once again, we face a hermeneutical circle that requires us to reaffirm the critical role of "prophecy" or "divination" in an extended, philosophical sense. As the Line makes clear, the power of *eikasia* enables philosophic education. The philosopher, however, does not make his way out of the cave single-handedly, for *eikasia* presupposes fundamental imaging relationships—relationships that, according to the Cave image, depend for their existence on prior human work. Whose work? Presumably not that of the many, "who don't know anything" about the noble and the beautiful (602b), or of the sophists, who pander to the many and refuse to distinguish between images and originals. The responsibility must lie with prophetic imagemakers, whose craft reflects and preserves within the tradition at least some part of the truth about the noble, the just, and the good.

Homer, Socrates suggests, is one of these prophetic imagemakers, who in his own way sustains the very possibility of philosophic education. Socrates singles out Homer as an authority on that which is godlike and the image of god in human beings: in shaping characters, the philosophic rulers of the Kallipolis would look both toward the Ideas and toward what exists in human beings, "and thus, mixing and blending the practices as ingredients, they would produce the image of man, taking hints from exactly that phenomenon in human beings *which Homer too* called godlike and the image of god" (501b; my italics). Homer, in other words, knows and gives voice in his poetry to the proper models for the philosophic ruler/craftsman's educational poems—models drawn from the Ideas as well as from human nature. Of course Socrates may still have reason to censure many other models Homer includes in his broad works. But it is undoubtedly the divine content of Homer's poems that makes Socrates feel the "friendship for Homer, and reverent shame [*aidōs*] before him" he mentions at the beginning of book 10 (595b).[7]

Socrates also alludes in the Cave image to Homer's knowledge of what is divine in humans and human life. Socrates favorably contrasts Homer with the other cave-dwellers when he asks whether the enlightened philosophic soul would envy the prisoners or "be affected as Homer says and want very much 'to be on the soil, a serf to another man, a portionless man' " (516d). Socrates' reference to what "Homer says" calls our attention to the knowledge Homer in particular possesses. Achilles, the literary character, can make the distinction between life on earth and the afterlife in Hades only because Homer, the author, knows the difference between these two things. Homer's knowledge of the difference between earth and Hades is thus a poetic image of the poet's own prophetic insight.

The prophetic poet sees that which is "god-like and the image of god," but it is the philosopher, not the poet, whom Socrates represents as leaving the cave and seeing the divine things themselves. In another dialogue, Socrates compares the poets to the Bacchae, worshipers of Dionysus who become possessed on drinking milk and honey (*Ion*, 534a). In the Cave Socrates partially repudiates his earlier criticisms of poetry by affirming a kind of divine inspiration that does not originate in the Olympian gods but does depend on a divine gift: the production and visibility of prophetic images is made possible by the firelight, and Socrates likens fire to the sun and calls the latter an offspring of the Good (517a-c).

Rather like Achilles when he addresses Odysseus after drinking the lamb's blood (*Odyssey*, 11.147-49), the prophetic poet is an intoxicated resident of the underworld. His peculiar, inspired intoxication allows him to utter meaningful images without any direct vision of the original objects. The metaphor of intoxication appropriately describes the prophetic poet's state, in that he forgets or is concealed from himself. For one thing, he directs or points human life but cannot clearly see that toward which he points. If a complete education involves a vision of the measures at which life points, as Socrates suggests, then the prophetic poet is not fully educated.

Finally, it is important that the poet sees himself first and foremost *as* a poet—that is, as a maker of images, and not just images of divine or godlike things but also of "all things human that have to do with virtue and vice" (598e). Socrates' basic criticism of Homer is therefore not that he does not provide good models for men but that the general educational effect of such models is diminished by the many worse models his poems contain as a result of his attempt to image the great multitude of things human and divine. Like the tragedians, Homer presents in his poems a variety of different and conflicting models, whose proper relationship his audiences are called on to see for themselves. But poems, like paintings, cannot explain their own meaning (cf. *Phaedrus*, 275d-e), and children—as well as most adults, in Socrates' view—"cannot judge what is a hidden sense and what is not" (378d).

The Philosophic Round Trip: Binding Together the Whole

In the Cave image the philosopher's love of wisdom leads him to the exterior of the cave. Glaucon agrees that the philosopher who has emerged from the cave "would prefer to undergo anything rather than live" as the prisoners do (516e). Why, then, does Socrates ask what would happen "if such a man [the philosopher] were to come down again and sit in the same seat" (516e)? Why, in short, does the philosopher return to the cave?

While the prophetic poet views the Whole only from the interior of the human realm, the philosopher, insofar as he stands outside of the cave, views the Whole from a perspective exterior to human life and political community. Each of these perspectives, however, is partial and incomplete: the Whole consists of originals *and* images, of the being of the Ideas and the Good *and* the becoming of the human realm, just as a fully human life consists of contemplation *and* practical and productive activity. The Cave image, however, indicates that the philosopher's *erōs* is sufficiently complex and comprehensive to attempt to encompass both the outer world and the cave. Just as the philosopher leaves the cave "by nature," we may infer that he returns to it in accordance with his own desires; although Socrates later states that the philosopher must be compelled to rule the cave-dwellers (520a), it is by no means clear that the philosopher must be compelled simply to re-enter the cave. Indeed, the philosopher's evidently voluntary return to the cave after he views the Ideas and the Good suggests that he is in the first place a human being, whose love of wisdom is not detached from his humanity but is, rather, the highest manifestation of his desire for a whole human life.

The philosopher may be reminded of his own complex nature by the Good. When the philosophic soul leaves the cave, he comes to see the Good as the source of the intelligibility of the Whole (516b-c). But Socrates repeatedly speaks of the Good as giving birth to its image, the sun, which is responsible for the generation and growth of visible things and so is an *archē* of life (506e, 508b, 517c). The Whole, in other words, is both intelligible and alive; it includes the soul as well as the Ideas. This means, however, that the philosopher's initial attempt to imitate and as much as possible make himself like the Ideas (500c) must give way to a recognition of the necessary and appropriate distinction between the soul and its intelligible objects. In exiting the cave, the philosopher sees living things and infers that the sun is the source of "the seasons and the years" that order their growth (516b); similarly, we are to understand that the Good makes visible the connection of the soul and the Ideas in a living, ordered Whole. The philosopher who ascends to the Good thus comes to see that while the soul and the Ideas are distinct, they are somehow united in a life in full bloom. Such a life is philosophical, but it is also human. In its wholeness, this life images the Good, or the wholeness of the Whole. To live a human life, however, is to speak and act within the arena of human, political community. It is, in short, to return to the cave.[8]

We asked at the beginning of this chapter why Socrates chose to speak about the Good by means of images. We are now in a position to observe that while nonimagistic speech runs the risk of conveying a false sense of clarity, precision, and finality, Socrates' philosophic images underscore the ceaseless character of the philosophic quest and emphasize the importance of dialogue.

As Socrates stresses, philosophic vision is problematic. Although the philosopher may divine along with Socrates that education is possible, he cannot know in advance that the "turning" toward being of *phronēsis*, the "eye" of the soul (518c*ff*), has been completed. In the terms of the Cave image, that turning is complete if the philosopher "sees" in the full "light" of the Good. But the philosopher has only his own vision to judge the light in which he sees—and the power of his vision to discern what is appropriate, fitting, or worthwhile and, in the broadest sense, to see what contributes to a good life depends on just this light. By analogy, the vision of a man who is in the dark, and who (like the prisoners in the cave) knows no other state, is "useless and harmful" (518e-19a), hence useless in judging the quality of the light in virtue of which he is able to see.

Because the philosopher cannot "step outside" of his own vision and compare his perceptions with that which truly is, he cannot know with certainty that his judgment is no longer distorted by his initial habituation to the shadows. This does not mean that education, or the improvement of vision, is impossible; on the contrary, simply to recognize that one now sees in a relatively better light than before is to acknowledge that education has in fact taken place. The deeper issue, however, is how one comes to see that one's vision requires improvement, and whether one can ever be sure that it does not. Socrates' answer to the latter question is clearly "No": any other response is antiphilosophical dogmatism. In Socrates' presentation of the matter, the philosopher can never be sure that his quest for wisdom has reached an end. The philosopher must always be prepared to check whether he is seeing things in the best light. In order to do so, the Socratic philosopher constantly seeks out philosophic dialogue, for in dialogue we in effect extend our vision by multiplying the eyes through which we see: philosophic conversation exposes one's vision of things to the scrutiny of another and allows one to see oneself through the eyes of the other. Finally, it should be obvious that while Socrates sees in others the opportunity to test his own understanding, he does not regard agreement as an adequate measure of truth: if everyone in the world already agreed with one, this would mean only that there were no more occasions for learning through dialogue.[9]

Applying the Socratic Image

The Sun, Line, and Cave emphasize the hermeneutically circular nature of philosophic inquiry as well as the circular or humanly comprehensive character of the philosophic journey. Perhaps most important, these images attempt to shed light on the possibility of philosophic education. In another dialogue, Socrates' interlocutor Meno formulates as a paradox the problem of how one can search for knowledge that one does not yet possess: "In what manner will you search, Socrates, for this thing about whose nature you know nothing? What sort of thing, among the things you know not, will you set before yourself as the object of your inquiry? Or even if you should happen to hit upon it directly, how will you know that this is the thing that you did not know?" (Plato, *Meno*, 80d). Socrates responds by denying Meno's premise: learning is to be understood, metaphorically, as the "recollection" of that with which we are in some sense *already* familiar (*Meno*, 81a*ff*). The Sun, Line, and Cave make the same point: the philosophical truth is already imagistically accessible in our prephilosophical experience. If the metaphorical character of these images does not entirely remove the mystery surrounding the accessibility of the truth within experience, is this not because the hermeuentical circle is itself genuinely mysterious? Indeed, the philosopher remains attached to the cavelike domain of human community not only because he delights in *all* of the truth, including images as well as originals (488a), but also because he recognizes that as a result of the ineradicably circular character of the quest for wisdom he will never cease to require dialogue.

The philosopher's return from the universality of the Ideas and the Good to the particularities of political community should serve as a model for our own interpretation of the *Republic*. Since the philosophical ascent and descent that takes place over the course of the *Republic* are phases of a single conversation, Socratic philosophizing actually seems to involve *repeated* "round trips" of the sort depicted in the Cave, or to consist in a shuttling, up-and-down movement of discourse whereby the examination through dialogue of the concrete texture of our experience opens up new approaches to the Ideas, and the exploration of these freshly opened avenues, in turn, sheds new light on the nature of our experience. Analogously, Socrates' otherwise abstract images of the Ideas and the Good stand in a reciprocal relationship to the concrete conversation of the *Republic*: neither the conversation nor the images will be fully intelligible unless they are woven together through the act of interpretation. While this interpretive weaving is necessarily imaginative, it is by no means equivalent to the creation of a work of fiction: the Sun, Line, and Cave illuminate the conversation precisely because they represent that which is already latent in it.

Finally, in stressing the unending character of the philosophic quest, the latter images decisively repudiate Socrates' earlier portrait of the philosophic rulers of the Kallipolis. Like Aristophanes' Cloud Cuckooland and the Kingdom of the Phaeacians, the Kallipolis is humanly impossible because it is too near the gods. It is for the same reason humanly undesirable: unlike Socrates, who pushes homeward with Odyssean tenacity, the philosophic ruler who longs simply to turn away from the human things (500b) has lost his way because he has forgotten that philosophy begins within and must return to the intermediate, human domain. The philosopher-kings are not genuine philosophers, nor could they become philosophers in a regime that forbids public, critical debate. Furthermore, they are erotically defective: the philosopher, as Socrates observes, "reach[es] out for the

Whole," including "everything divine and human"; like Socrates, he is "greedy" not only for originals, but for images as well (486a, 488a). Having gone through the images of the Sun, Line, and Cave, Socrates and his attentive readers are already well on their way home from Glaucon's fantastic regime.

10

Coming Home? Philosophy and Necessity in the Myth of Er

After completing his account of the Kallipolis in book 7, Socrates turns to an exploration of the reciprocal relationship within actual political communities between *nomos* and human character. In particular, he recounts in books 8 and 9 the seemingly inevitable transformation of the truly aristocratic regime (the Kallipolis) and the aristocratic soul through timocracy, oligarchy, and democracy into tyranny. Socrates' narrative follows the soul and the regime as they move jointly through a series of distinct erotic orientations that are both registered in and fostered by political participation and the aims of public life.

The basic thesis of books 8 and 9 is already familiar from the Cave image: human dispositions are formed by a shifting tide of psychological and political forces as if by natural necessity. Socrates' account, which begins with the Nuptial Number, emphasizes that although our erotic natures bear the impress of custom and convention they are never wholly mastered by *nomos*. *Erōs* exists by nature and so is prior to *nomos*. It is ultimately stronger than *nomos* as well, for it is somehow a dynamic, eruptive power as well as a malleable substratum.

In calling attention to the complex, recalcitrant character of *erōs*, Socrates makes it clear that in any regime, including the Kallipolis, philosophy alone is the means whereby one may "win one's own soul," if by "soul" we mean an independent center of responsible action. Only the philosopher who emerges from the cave takes personal responsibility for the intelligent ordering of his own soul. What is more, regardless of the arrangement of the cave's public spaces, only philosophic education is capable of bringing good order to the "interior space" of the psyche: whereas the philosopher is said to have a vivid paradigm of the Ideas *within* his soul, the nonphilosophical citizens of the Kallipolis, who remain within the cave, have images of the Ideas "painted" *onto* their souls by the philosophic rulers (484c, 501a-c).

Socrates returns to the problem of the soul's order in the Myth of Er, in which he makes explicit the superficiality of all nonphilosophical "education." While in Hades, Er observes the lottery of lives (617d*ff*), wherein each soul chooses the life it will lead in its next incarnation. There, Er sees a soul that has come down from heaven because it had lived virtuously in its former life. Yet the virtuous behavior of this particular soul was the result of forces external to itself: it had lived in an "orderly regime"—a regime that in this crucial respect resembles the Kallipolis—and had participated in virtue "by habit, without philosophy" (619c-d). Because its virtue was always only skin-deep, this soul is now swayed by unchecked "folly [*aphrosunē*] and gluttony" and so jumps at the chance to possess "the greatest tyranny" without first reading the fine print about the evils it is fated to undergo in its future existence (619b-c).

Far from being a "radiant" vision that "makes my soul out to be a pure, non-composite intellectual substance" (Nussbaum, 223), the Myth of Er dramatizes the profound paradox involved in choosing to lead a philosophic life—a paradox rooted in the formation of one's soul through the habituation of appetite and emotion as well as intellect. While the Myth of Er explicitly connects philosophy with personal salvation through its tale of the lottery of lives, it also formulates in the sharpest possible terms the problem of how it is possible, as the myth urges, to become philosophical. There are really two profound problems here. First, how can the soul overcome the psychic "necessities" that militate against philosophy? Second, how is it conceivable that one begins at some time to be philosophical? The myth teaches that we need philosophy in order to make intelligent and responsible choices about the lives we lead and the condition of our souls. But how can one meaningfully choose a life of philosophy? Must one not already have taken responsibility for oneself, and so already be philosophical, in order to "choose" to live philosophically?

Before we return to the Myth of Er, let us briefly examine the image of the soul that Socrates sets forth at the end of book 9 (588b-89b), which introduces the problems I have raised by reopening the issue of *erōs*.

ERŌS AS MONSTER AND SAVIOR

Whereas in book 4 Socrates confined *erōs* to the irrational, appetitive part of the soul (439d), he begins book 9 by admitting that the kinds and numbers of appetites have not yet been adequately distinguished (571a). In particular, each of the three parts of the soul mentioned in book 4 is now said to have its own appetites (*epithumiai*) and corresponding pleasures (580d). Thus the spirited part loves victory and honor, and "the part by which a human being learns"—a part now especially associated with *phronēsis* and *nous* (582d, 583a-b, 586d)— loves learning and wisdom (581b). Socrates' extension of desire to the soul as a whole is necessary for his subsequent demonstration that the philosophic life is the most pleasurable life, and that the pleasures of men not characterized by *phronēsis* are "shadow paintings" and "phantom images" (582a*ff*, 583b, 586b-c). At the same time, this extension of desire allows us to interpret the complex image of the soul with which Socrates concludes book 9 as a symbolic expression of the polytropic, conflicted nature of *erōs* itself.

Socrates represents as a human being the part of the soul that learns, the spirited part as a lion, and the epithumetic part, on the model of "the Chimaera, and Scylla, and Cerberus," as "a many-colored, many-headed beast that has a ring of heads of tame and savage beasts and can change them and make them all grow from itself" (588c).[1] The latter image reflects the savage, lawless character of tyrannical *erōs*, which even in the ordered, philosophic soul sometimes stalks the imaginative landscape of the mind in dreams (571c*ff*). In the just soul, the human being controls the many-headed beast with the aid of the lion as an ally, "starving" the savage heads and "nourishing" the tame heads, whereas in the unjust and tyrannical soul the beast and the lion together starve the human being (588e-89b).

Socrates' image makes clear the inadequacy of the accounts of moderation and justice in book 4, both as descriptions of the soul and the city. In the first place, the multifarious and protean nature of the epithumetic part of the soul makes highly problematic a straightforward enumeration of the soul's elements. Second, and most important, it seems ludicrous to expect that the many-headed monster would willingly accept being ruled or could be bound by affection (*philia*) with the other parts of the soul. Socrates' suggestion to this effect is highly paradoxical, as is his depiction of the human being as a farmer who merely "nourishes" the tame heads and "hinders from growing" the savage ones (589b). The image is overwhelmingly violent and polemic, not pastoral or agricultural: it seems clear that the human, who is smaller "by far" than the lion (588d), must ally with the lion and fight tooth and nail if he is to have any chance at all against the monster.[2]

Read as a political image, the present passage confirms Aristotle's impression that the Auxiliaries are essentially an occupying army within the ostensibly just regime (cf. 415d-e). Read as a psychological image, the passage suggests that the soul is a battlefield of desires, in which moderation and justice as defined in book 4 are out of the question. Force and conquest now replace *philia* or concord as a model of the soul's internal relationships. Whether the soul is human or less than human, in turn, depends on the erotic strength of the "human," philosophical part—"the part of the soul that learns"—in relation to the other, bestial parts. No political regime can substitute for philosophy in nourishing and strengthening this distinctively human *erōs*, for Er's story of the lottery of lives shows that even in a well-orderedregime the human part of the soul remains excessively weak in relation to the many-headed beast.

The preceding analysis, however, merely underscores the paradoxical character of Socrates' image. If sheer strength is all, then even enforced decency—let alone philosophy—is impossible: no human is simply stronger than a lion, much less a monster. In other words, something not altogether unlike "farming" and "friendship"—if we understand these generally as images of a peaceful relationship between parts of the soul—must be possible after all, since the human part of the soul cannot rule by force alone. As in the political community, persuasion must accompany force (cf. 327c-28a). On the other hand, reasoned argument (logos) is of no use in ruling the epithumetic or nonrational part of the soul (*alogiston*: 439d), although it may perhaps be of use in helping to "tame" the "lion" of *thumos*, which in its nature somehow stands in between the other two parts (cf. 439e*ff*). To master the soul as a whole, then, the human being in us must have recourse to a kind of persuasion that is neither simply rational nor irrational and that speaks directly to *erōs*, relaxing some erotic longings while arousing others. In brief, the human being in us needs music.

We may summarize the main implications of Socrates' image as follows. One's hope for a well-ordered soul—to the extent that the word *order* may meaningfully apply to the psychic menagerie Socrates describes—rests on genuine education or philosophy. Philosophic education, however, does not proceed by argument alone, for the power of logos over the soul rests in part on the prior work of music. Socrates' image of the soul thus reinforces his earlier claim that "logos mixed with music . . . alone, when it is present, dwells within the one possessing it as a savior of virtue throughout life" (549b; cf. 548b-c). Yet philosophic music mixed with logos is not sufficient to make philosophers out of those unfitted by nature for the quest for wisdom (cf. 485a-87a). In some sense, then, the soul of the potential philosopher, prior to its education, must *already* be constituted and arranged in such a way as to favor the human element as much as possible, and to be fully open to the ordering influence of philosophic music and logos.

Socrates' image of the soul calls our attention to several perplexing issues. What accounts for the prephilosophic constitution and arrangement of the soul? Since the image suggests that the human part of the soul is naturally at a disadvantage in relation to its beastly com-petitors, to what extent, if any, can we expect individuals to be responsible for educating themselves and leading good lives? Does Socrates mean to suggest that the possibility of philosophy itself, like that of the Kallipolis, ultimately depends on rare good luck or "divine chance" (592a)? Precisely these questions are taken up in the Myth of Er, Socrates' recantation of his own philosophic "tale of Alkinoos" (614b)—the Kallipolis myth of perfectly wise philosophic rulers.

THE LOTTERY OF LIVES AND THE PARADOX OF PHILOSOPHY

The Myth of Er (614b-21b) is large and metaphorically complex. We are here concerned with the philosophical implications of only one aspect of the myth, that of the lottery of lives (617d-21b).

Everyman is a medieval moral play in which Death, acting in the service of God, summons Everyman to give an account of his life.[3] The Myth of Er, a man of the race of Pamphylon ("Everytribe," 614b), is the Platonic ancestor of all such stories about our universal and inevitable fate. This story is appropriately situated at the end of the philosophic odyssey dramatized in the *Republic*, since Er's journey brings him "home" to the center of the universe, the place from which each soul starts out in its journey through life and to which it ultimate-ly returns.

At the center of the universe there is a great column of light, as well as the "spindle of Necessity" around which the cosmos revolves in concentric circles (616b-17c). Since it is in this location that the lottery of lives takes place, the myth encourages us to compare the circular motion of the cosmos as a whole with the movement of each soul as it passes through the continuous cycle of reincarnation. While Er relates that the spindle "by which all the revolutions are turned" revolves "in the lap" of the goddess of Necessity (616c, 617b), he does not actually say that Necessity herself turns the spindle. He adds, however, that Lachesis, Clotho, and Atropon—daughters of Necessity, and the Fates, respectively, of past, present, and future—join in turning the circles, "ceasing from time to time" (617c). We may note that of the Fates Lachesis has the most influence over the revolution of the cosmos, for she alone assists in moving both the outer and inner circles (617c). In general, the rather mysterious details of Er's account suggest that the role of Necessity in the motion of the cosmos is important but ambiguous. The most we can say with confidence is that fate plays some part in this motion and that the past is in this respect more influential than either the present or the future.[4]

Er's account of the influence of necessity over human life is similarly ambiguous. The pre-Socratic philosopher Heracleitus maintained that "character [*ēthos*] is destiny [*daimōn*] for a human being" (Freeman, 32: frag. 119). Greek grammar allows one to read either "*ēthos* is *daimōn*" or "*daimōn* is *ēthos*," meaning either that character—who one is—determines one's lot in life, or that *daimōn* in the sense that Er describes—a semidivine "guardian" and "fulfiller" of one's lot in life (620d-e), hence one's predestined "fate"—determines who one is. Heracleitus is silent, perhaps intentionally, about which alternative he prefers. Indeed, it has recently been argued that Greek tragedy is essentially an exploration of the ambiguity captured in Heracleitus's claim (Vernant, 1988, 37). It is striking that just this distinctively tragic ambiguity stands at the philosophical and dramatic center of the Myth of Er.

At first sight Er's narrative seems to imply that the soul is responsible for its own destiny. The lottery is open to souls that have come down from heaven or up from earth, having been rewarded or punished for the justice or injustice of their former lives (614c-16a). It is conducted under the auspices of Lachesis, "Distributor of Lots." A spokesman or "prophet" (*prophētēs*) takes from Lachesis lots and "paradigms of lives" (617d). The lots determine the order in which the souls are to choose their lives, but there are many more lives to choose from (including animal lives and "all the varieties of human lives") than there are souls present (617e-18a). It is important to observe that the lives are called "paradigms," which indicates that although each life is in some ways different from all others, individual human lives are not unique in their essentials: they may be grouped together with other lives and distinguished from the rest according to kinds. The myth thus suggests that in general the same variety of different *sorts* of lives is always open to human beings, regardless of the era in which one is born—a point underscored by the fact that Lachesis, the Fate who "sing[s] . . . of what has been" (617c), oversees the lottery. Furthermore, it is our ability to study and compare the kinds of lives from which we must choose that makes plausible Socrates' plea that we devote ourselves to philosophy so that we can choose intelligently (618b-19b).

Socrates implicitly likens himself to the prophet who conducts the lottery: while in the *Clouds* the character of Socrates looked down on Strepsiades from his basket and called him a "creature of a day" (*Clouds*, 223), the prophet ascends a "high platform" and uses the same term (*ephēmere*) in addressing the souls (617d). Socrates' plea for philosophy also echoes the prophet's warnings. "A *daimōn* will not select you," the prophet tells the souls, "but you will choose a *daimōn*. . . . Virtue is without a master; as he holds her in esteem or dishonor, each will have more or less of her. You bear responsibility in making your choice; god is blameless" (617d-e). The prophet later warns all against carelessness and explains that even the man who comes forward last may find a satisfactory life if he chooses "with intelligence [*nous*]" (619b).

The prophet clearly regards souls as beings more substantial and responsible than the half-witted shades that populate Homer's Hades. Furthermore, the preceding details of the lottery of lives suggest that the influence over one's life of forces beyond one's control is restricted to the role played by chance in determining the order of lots (cf. 619d) but that chance is not decisive in determining one's fate. Yet other details, particularly those that are meant to explain the many poor choices Er witnesses, imply that necessity, as distinguished from mere accident or chance, *is* decisive in one's choice of life. Socrates observes that the selections of the various souls were "pitiable, and laughable, and amazing," and were made "for the most part according to the habituation of their former life" (620a). Thus many of those who rushed into poor choices, including the soul that picked out "the greatest tyranny," had come down from heaven and were "unpracticed in labors," whereas the souls that came up from their punishment beneath the earth were in general much more careful (619c). For this reason, "there was an exchange of evils and goods for most of the souls" (619d).

The latter passages suggest that a soul's capacity to listen to the forewarnings of the prophet and to act in accordance with his words is for the most part determined by prior habituation (as is also implied by the etymological connection between *ēthos* and *ethos*, or "character" and "habit"). This implication is confirmed by Socrates' comment that "an ordering of the soul was not in them [the paradigms of lives], due to the necessity that a soul become different according to the life it chooses" (618b). In other words, the life one chooses to live necessarily impresses itself on one's soul in a way that affects the soul's future choices. (We should note in this connection that the lottery operates on the principle that "all sales are final": the Fates attach to each soul as a *daimōn* the lot it has chosen, so that the "threads" of its destiny— a metaphor that links the act of choice with the "spinning" motion of the cosmos—are "irreversible" [620e].) Seen in this light, the figure of Lachesis takes on new significance: who one is and will be depends on who one already was. Who one was, in turn, apparently has to do with the initial constitution or nature of the soul as well as the kinds of lives one has led. Some such distinction is at any rate implicit in Socrates' remark that an ordering of the soul is not included in the paradigms: if all souls were the same in nature, there would be no reason not to include an ordering of the soul in each paradigm, since each life would affect every soul in the same way. Socrates implies instead that different souls will be influenced in different ways by the same circumstances. Perhaps most important, his comment that souls choose "for the most part" according to the habituation of their former lives, and that "most" of the souls Er saw exchanged evils and goods, suggests that a few souls learn well from their experiences, whereas a few do not learn at all. The latter, along with all the rest—the many souls that neither exchange goods for goods nor evils for evils but swing back and forth between the two—are apparently constrained by the necessity of their own natures and the prior ordering of their souls to "choose" to live as they do. The soul that selects the greatest tyranny is evidently not as unreasonable as it first seems to be in blaming "chance, *daimōns*, and anything rather than itself" for its bad choice (619c).

Whereas the prophet asserts that *ēthos* is *daimōn*, the Myth of Er seems to teach that *daimōn* is *ēthos*, and in particular that one cannot meaningfully "choose" to live a philosophic life. But this is not all, for the myth challenges this teaching in and through the very act of articulating it. In selecting its future life, Socrates tells us, the soul remembers nothing prior to its previous life. In particular, it has no recollection of the lottery of lives in which it chose its last life, because prior to each incarnation the soul is compelled—perhaps by the intense heat of the place—to drink from the river of Carelessness in the plain of Forgetfulness (*Lēthē*), and in so doing it "forgets everything" (621a-b). This requirement has profound implications, for if the soul could reflect on its past experiences and the experiences of other souls in the lottery of lives it would be able to see beyond the habitual horizons of its former life and might therefore make its selection more prudently. Yet Er himself, who was told "to listen and to look at everything" but was forbidden to drink from the river (614d, 621b), was granted precisely such an opportunity. Furthermore, Er's "prophetic" message allows *us* to see the lottery of lives and hear the words of the prophet, and thereby potentially to overcome the necessity of forgetfulness and the constraints of habituation that hold sway over other souls. The way is thus open to us to follow the heartening example of the soul of Odysseus, which, "having recovered from the love of honor by means of the memory of its former labors," looked "for a long time" through the paradigms and "with effort" chose best, although it chose last (620c-d).

THE MYSTERY OF PHILOSOPHY

The Myth of Er does not answer the questions it raises about the origins of philosophy and the overcoming of necessity. Perhaps we cannot fully answer these questions, so that Socrates is prudent to leave these issues shrouded in mystery. It would follow that complete self-knowledge or wisdom is inaccessible; philosophy never finally becomes *sophia*. The reader will recall, however, that we reached the same conclusion in the last chapter in reflecting on the mysteries of the hermeneutical circle and the philosopher's unceasing need for dialogue. Like the Sun, Line, and Cave, the Myth of Er is ultimately optimistic: it confirms the possibility of learning and holds out hope to each of us that we ourselves may be capable of undergoing a philosophic education.

To be persuaded by the Myth of Er is to be persuaded by Socrates (621c), for the Myth is Socrates' tale. Socrates evidently hopes to have convinced Glaucon merely to cling "adamantly" (*adamantiños*: 618e-19a) to the quest for justice, and thereby to imitate Adeimantus's morally solid nature (cf. 616c, where the spindle of Necessity is said to be composed *ex adamantos*, "of adamant"). Insofar as we readers are persuaded by Socrates, however, the Myth in several ways turns our attention back toward the dialogue that has just been completed. In recounting the *Republic*, Socrates, like the prophet of whom Er speaks, has laid out the paradigms of lives—including those of himself and all of his companions—among which we must choose. Furthermore, even if the Myth of Er does not explain how choice is *possible*, we may find that the dialogue itself dramatically demonstrates its *actuality*. At the very least, the spectacle of Socrates' companions pursuing or failing to pursue the opportunity of philosophic conversation will help to show what sorts of souls we must possess if we are to become philosophers. In fine, it is in approaching the dialogue carefully and intelligently, and in thinking through the paradigmatic speeches and deeds of its characters at length and with effort, that we may best imitate Odysseus, Er, and Socrates himself.

Notes

1. Plato's Athens

1. Plato, *Apology of Socrates*, 38a. Plato's works are hereafter cited in text by title and standard (Stephanus) page numbers. Unless otherwise indicated, all translations of passages from dialogues other than the *Republic* are my own. References to Bloom's notes in *The Republic of Plato* henceforth appear in the text, as do references to Adam's Greek text and notes.

2. For an introduction to ancient Greek religion, see Jean-Pierre Vernant, "Greek Religion," in *The Encyclopedia of Religion*, vol. 6, ed. Mircea Eliade (New York: Macmillan, 1987), 99-118; hereafter cited in text. The ritual aspect of Greek religion included making sacrifices and presenting votive offerings to the gods, engaging in initiation rites and processions, and the like.

3. Herodotus, *The Persian Wars*, trans. George Rawlinson (New York: The Modern Library, 1942), 2.53.

4. *Hecuba*, 488-92, in *The Complete Greek Tragedies*, 4 vols., ed. David Grene and Richmond Lattimore (Chicago: University of Chicago Press, 1959); *Clouds*, 367, in *Four Texts on Socrates: Plato's "Euthyphro," "Apology," and "Crito" and Aristophanes' "Clouds,"* trans. Thomas G. West and Grace Starry West (Ithaca, N.Y.: Cornell University Press, 1984). References to the other plays of Aristophanes are drawn from *Aristophanes*, 3 vols., trans. Benjamin Bickley Rogers, Loeb Classical Library (Cambridge, Mass.: Harvard University Press, 1924). All Greek dramas are hereafter cited in text.

5. The following paragraphs recapitulate some of the major points of chapter 1 of Paul A. Rahe, *Republics Ancient and Modern: Classical Republicanism and the American Revolution* (Chapel Hill: University of North Carolina Press, 1992), 28-54.

6. Thucydides, in *Thucydides Translated into English*, trans. Benjamin Jowett (Oxford: Clarendon Press, 1881), 2.34-47; hereafter cited in text.

7. *Aristotle: The Politics*, trans. Carnes Lord (Chicago: University of Chicago Press, 1984), 1253a11-18; hereafter cited in text as *Politics*.

8. Concerning Alcibiades, see the Chronology; Plutarch's *Alcibiades* in Plutarch, *The Rise and Fall of Athens*, trans. Ian Scott-Kilvert (Harmondsworth: Penguin, 1960); and Jacob Howland, "Socrates and Alcibiades: Eros, Piety, and Politics," *Interpretation* 18, no. 1 (1990): 63-90.

9. Aristotle, *Nicomachean Ethics*, trans. Martin Ostwald (Indianapolis: Bobbs-Merrill, 1962), 1095b26-29, 1159a17-21. The latter passage connects the love of honor with the love of pleasure, the most common object of desire (see 1095b19-22); hereafter cited in text as *Ethics*.

2. The *Republic* and the Origins of Political Philosophy

1. Cicero, *Tusculan Disputations*, trans. J. E. King (Cambridge, Mass.: Harvard University Press, 1927), 5.10-11.

2. Leo Strauss, *The City and Man* (1964; Chicago: University of Chicago Press, 1978), 55.

3. Unless the context indicates otherwise, "Socrates" hereafter refers to the character of Socrates in the Platonic dialogues.

3. Critical Provocations

1. Alfred North Whitehead, *Process and Reality, Corrected Edition*, ed. David Ray Griffin and Donald W. Sherburne (New York: Free Press, 1978), 2.1.1.

2. Unless another title is specified, all Stephanus page numbers cited in the text hereafter refer to the *Republic*.

3. Karl Popper, *The Open Society and Its Enemies*, vol. 1 (1943; Princeton: Princeton University Press, 1966), 42; hereafter cited in text.

4. Friedrich Nietzsche, *Beyond Good and Evil: Prelude to a Philosophy of the Future*, trans. Walter Kaufmann (New York: Random House, Vintage Books, 1966), 13.

5. Friedrich Nietzsche, *On the Advantage and Disadvantage of History for Life*, trans. Peter Preuss (Indianapolis: Hackett Publishing, 1980), 10, 39.

6. Friedrich Nietzsche, *The Birth of Tragedy*, in *The Birth of Tragedy and The Case of Wagner*, trans. Walter Kaufmann (New York: Random House, Vintage Books, 1967), 91; hereafter cited in text.

7. See "The Problem of Socrates," in *Twilight of the Idols*, included in *The Portable Nietzsche*, trans. Walter Kaufmann (New York: Penguin Books, 1976), 473-79.

8. Martha C. Nussbaum, *The Fragility of Goodness: Luck and Ethics in Greek Tragedy and Philosophy* (Cambridge: Cambridge University Press, 1986).

9. For an alternative and highly sympathetic approach to Plato's political philosophy, consult the medieval Islamic and Jewish interpretive tradition, including Averroes, *Averroes on Plato's "Republic,"* trans. Ralph Lerner (Ithaca, N.Y.: Cornell University Press, Agora Paperback Editions, 1974), and selections from Alfarabi and Maimonides in *Medieval Political Philosophy*, ed. Ralph Lerner and Muhsin Mahdi (1963; Ithaca, N.Y.: Cornell University Press, Agora Paperback Editions, 1972).

4. Interpreting Plato

1. Diogenes Laertius, *Lives of Eminent Philosophers*, vol. 1, ed. and trans. R. D. Hicks, Loeb Classical Library (Cambridge, Mass.: Harvard University Press, 1938), 1:3.5; hereafter cited in text.

Notes

2. In "Comedy in Callipolis: Animal Imagery in the *Republic*" (*American Political Science Review* 72, no. 3 [1978]: 888-901; hereafter cited in text) Arlene W. Saxenhouse notes that "there are at least 20 uses of some form of *geloios* ["laughable"] within the first 35 Stephanus pages of the fifth book [of the *Republic*]" (895n20).

3. See *Ancilla to the Pre-Socratic Philosophers*, trans. Kathleen Freeman (Cambridge, Mass.: Harvard University Press, 1977), 47, 127-29; hereafter cited in text.

4. Valuable discussions of the dialogue form may be found in Jacob Klein, *A Commentary on Plato's "Meno"* (Chapel Hill: University of North Carolina Press, 1965), 3-31 (hereafter cited in text); Drew A. Hyland, "Why Plato Wrote Dialogues," *Philosophy and Rhetoric* 1 (1968): 38-50; and Charles L. Griswold, Jr., "Plato's Metaphilosophy: Why Plato Wrote Dialogues," in *Platonic Writings, Platonic Readings*, ed. Charles L. Griswold, Jr. (New York: Routledge, 1988), 143-67 (hereafter cited in text).

5. Froma Zeitlin calls Greek tragedy "the epistemological genre par excellence, which continually calls into question what we know and how we think we know it" ("Playing the Other: Theater, Theatricality, and the Feminine in Greek Drama," in *Nothing To Do with Dionysus?*, ed. John J. Winkler and Froma I. Zeitlin [Princeton: Princeton University Press, 1990], 78). A similar approach to tragedy can be found in Jean-Pierre Vernant, "Tensions and Ambiguities in Greek Tragedy," in Jean-Pierre Vernant and Pierre Vidal-Naquet, *Myth and Tragedy in Ancient Greece,* trans. Janet Lloyd (New York: Zone Books, 1988), 29-48; hereafter cited in text.

6. Olympiodorus, *Commentary on the "First Alcibiades" of Plato*, ed. L. G. Westerink (Amsterdam: North-Holland Publishing, 1956), 2.71-72.

7. Saxenhouse (890-91) stresses in particular the connection between the *Republic* and the *Birds*. On the relationship between *Republic*, book 5, and the *Assemblywomen*, see Bloom 1968, 467-68n5, and "Aristophanes and Plato: A Response to Hall," in Allan Bloom, *Giants and Dwarfs* (New York: Simon & Schuster, 1990), 162-76. For a detailed discussion of the *Republic* as Plato's response to Aristophanes' *Clouds*, see Mary P. Nichols, *Socrates and the Political Community: An Ancient Debate* (Albany: State University of New York Press, 1987).

8. See Jacob Howland, "Re-reading Plato: The Problem of Platonic Chronology," *Phoenix* 45, no. 3 (1991): 189-214.

9. Charles Segal "'The Myth Was Saved': Reflections on Homer and the Mythology of Plato's *Republic*," *Hermes* 106, no. 2 (1978): 315-36; hereafter cited in text.

10. Compare Nussbaum's counterclaim that the myths of the *Republic* "are not essential to the philosophical argument; they come after it and reinforce it" (Nussbaum, 131). Some of the criticisms of Nussbaum's approach to Plato that I have touched on in this chapter are amplified and extended in David L. Roochnik, "The Tragic Philosopher: A Critique of Martha

Nussbaum," *Ancient Philosophy* 8 (Fall 1988): 285-95, and the review of *The Fragility of Goodness* by Charles L. Griswold, Jr., in the *American Scholar* 57, no. 2 (1988): 314-20. See also Jacob Howland, "Philosophy as Dialogue: Charles L. Griswold, Jr.'s *Self-Knowledge in Plato's 'Phaedrus,' " Reason Papers* 17 (1992): 113-34, which includes further discussion of the relationship between Aristophanes and Plato and the interpretive implications of traditional assumptions about Platonic chronology.

5. The Philosophic Odyssey

1. This point has recently been emphasized in Zdravko Planinc, *Plato's Political Philosophy: Prudence in the "Republic" and the "Laws"* (Columbia: University of Missouri Press, 1991); hereafter cited in text.

2. Aristotle, *Poetics*, trans. W. H. Fyfe, Loeb Classical Library (Cambridge, Mass.: Harvard University Press, 1932), 1453a30-37.

3. On the original tragic theme of Mystery initiation, see Richard Seaford, "Dionysiac Drama and the Dionysiac Mysteries," *Classical Quarterly* 31, no. 2 (1981): 252-75.

4. Bruce Rosenstock, "Rereading the *Republic*," *Arethusa* 16, nos. 1 and 2 (1983): 226; hereafter cited in text.

5. Given the great length of the *Republic* and the fact that Socrates omits parts of the conversation (e.g., 342c-d and 350c-d), the discussion must have taken all night.

6. On the mathematical and poetical inflections of *erōs* and the relationship between the *Symposium* and the *Republic*, see Stanley Rosen, "The Role of Eros in Plato's *Republic*," *Review of Metaphysics* 18 (1965): 452-75.

7. Socrates engages in a similar transformation of the mythical tradition in Plato's *Euthyphro* (see 6a with 6d-e).

8. Diskin Clay stresses this incompleteness in "Reading the *Republic*," in *Platonic Writings, Platonic Readings*, 19-33.

9. See Eva Brann, "The Music of the *Republic*," 8-9, in *Four Essays on Plato's "Republic": Saint John's Review* 39, nos. 1 and 2 (1989-90): 1-103; hereafter cited in text.

10. Xenophon, *Memorabilia*, 1.2.12*ff*, in Xenophon, vol. 4, *Memorabilia, Oeconomicus, Symposium, Apology*, trans. E. C. Marchant and O. J. Todd, Loeb Classical Library (Cambridge, Mass.: Harvard University Press, 1923). On the date of Cephalus's death, see W. K. C. Guthrie, *A History of Greek Philosophy*, vol. 4 (Cambridge: Cambridge University Press, 1975), 437. On the deaths of Polemarchus and Niceratus, see Lysias, Orations 12 and 18, in *Lysias*, ed. W. R. M. Lamb, Loeb Classical Library (Cambridge, Mass.: Harvard University Press, 1930).

11. A thorough account of what is known of the Eleusinian Mysteries may be found in Walter Burkert, *Homo Necans: The Anthropology of Ancient*

Greek Sacrificial Ritual and Myth, trans. Peter Bing (Berkeley: University of California Press, 1983), 248-97.

12. For the connection between philosophy and religious initiation before Plato, see especially the poem of Parmenides in Freeman, 41-46. Plato frequently uses the image of Mystery initiation to represent the turning of the soul toward philosophy: see *Phaedrus,* 244*aff*; *Phaedo,* 69c; *Symposium,* 210*aff*, 215c; and *Gorgias,* 493a-b, 497c.

13. Alexander Heidel, *The Gilgamesh Epic and Old Testament Parallels* (Chicago: University of Chicago Press, 1946), 1.

14. On the latter associations, see Douglas Frame's *The Myth of Return in Early Greek Epic* (New Haven, Conn.: Yale University Press, 1978). On the Phaeacians as a bridge between the realms of "fantasy" and "reality," see Charles Segal, "The Phaeacians and the Symbolism of Odysseus' Return," *Arion* 1, no. 1 (1962): 17-64. On Odysseus's transitions, see Charles Segal, "Transition and Ritual in Odysseus' Return," in the Norton Critical Edition of the *Odyssey,* ed. Albert Cook (New York: Norton, 1974), 465-86. All of the preceding are hereafter cited in text.

15. Homer, *Odyssey,* 2 vols., trans. A. T. Murray, Loeb Classical Library (Cambridge, Mass.: Harvard University Press, 1919), 1.5. References to the *Iliad* are drawn from the Loeb edition, 2 vols., trans. A. T. Murray (Cambridge, Mass.: Harvard University Press, 1924). On Odysseus's quest to win his identity, see G. E. Dimock, Jr., "The Name of Odysseus," in the Norton Critical Edition of the *Odyssey,* 406-24. All of the preceding are hereafter cited in text.

16. Like Er, Odysseus subsequently awakens from his voyage as from a dream (*Odyssey,* 13.187-89; cf. Segal 1962, 31). For a different reading of the Odyssean subtext, see Planinc. Planinc unfortunately distorts Homer in attempting to interpret the *Republic* and the *Laws* together as an extended philosophic "homecoming." He is forced to argue that the latter dialogues "are no more at odds with one another than the first half of the *Odyssey* is at odds with the second. Odysseus' wanderings came to an end when he arrived at the land of the Phaiakians" (273).

17. It is noteworthy that Aristophanes emphasizes Heracles' huge bodily appetites and dull intellect: see *Frogs,* 503-18; *Birds,* 1579-1692.

18. In "Plato's Pharmacy" (in *Disseminations,* trans. Barbara Johnson [Chicago: University of Chicago Press, 1981], 61-171; hereafter cited in text) Jacques Derrida explores Plato's presentation of philosophy as an antidote to the "poison" of sophistry and as a means to conquer "death." Derrida's fascinating and provocative essay attempts to show that the Platonic distinction between philosophy and sophistry cannot be maintained. Thoughtful criticisms of "Plato's Pharmacy" that attempt to defend the latter distinction may be found in Griswold 1988 and in "Platonic Reconstruction," chapter 2 of Stanley Rosen, *Hermeneutics as Politics* (Oxford: Oxford University Press, 1987), 50-86.

6. A Host of Challenges

1. On the ambiguity of Socrates' educational practice, see Plato, *Sophist*, 226b-31b. Socratic philosophizing is connected with theft at Aristophanes, *Clouds*, 177-79, 719, 856-59, 1498 (cf. *Theaetetus*, 169a-c). See also the profound characterization of Socratic pedagogy in Søren Kierkegaard, *Philosophical Fragments*, 9ff, in *Philosophical Fragments/Johannes Climacus*, vol. 7 of *Kierkegaard's Writings*, ed. and trans. Howard V. Hong and Edna H. Hong (Princeton: Princeton University Press, 1985).

2. On the philosophic significance of Cleitophon, see Plato's *Cleitophon* as well as David L. Roochnik, "The Riddle of the *Cleitophon*," *Ancient Philosophy* 4 (1984): 132-45.

7. Socratic Mythmaking and Philosophic Pedagogy

1. Hesiod, *Works and Days*, 109-120, in *Hesiod, the Homeric Hymns, and Homerica*, trans. Hugh G. Evelyn-White, Loeb Classical Library (Cambridge, Mass.: Harvard University Press, 1914); hereafter cited in text.

2. A thorough discussion of *paideia* can be found in Rahe, 105-35.

3. Socrates' approach to these problems is sensibly explored in Carl Page, "The Truth about Lies in Plato's *Republic*," *Ancient Philosophy* 11 (1991): 1-33.

8. A Comic Tale of Two Cities

1. Socrates' criticisms of the traditional theology recall those of Xenophanes and Parmenides: see Freeman, 20-24, 41-46.

2. On Odysseus's cowardice, see the *Iliad*, 8.90-98, and Sophocles, *Ajax*, 1-88. Odysseus's nature is best illustrated in the placement of his ship on the beach at Troy: it is dead center, in the most protected position, while the ships of Achilles and Ajax are exposed on the extreme wings *(Iliad*, 11.5-9). On Achilles' truth-telling, see the *Iliad*, 9.308-14.

3. Giovanni Comotti, *Music in Greek and Roman Culture*, trans. Rosaria V. Munson (Baltimore: Johns Hopkins University Press, 1989), 25; hereafter cited in text.

4. An excellent commentary on the educational significance of music can be found in Allan Bloom, *The Closing of the American Mind* (New York: Simon & Schuster, 1987), 68-81.

5. On the role of pederasty in Greek life, see Rahe, 128-35. On Glaucon's homoerotic nature, cf. 474e-75a.

6. Compare Nietzsche's discussion in *The Birth of Tragedy* of the origin of poetry from a "musical mood," as opposed to conceptual understanding of the sort embodied in Socrates' models (49; cf. 55).

7. Interestingly, the Athenian Stranger in Plato's *Laws* (663e-64a) mentions the Cadmus myth as an example of the way in which lawgivers can persuade men of virtually anything.

8. Cf. Aristophanes' *Lysistrata* (411 B.C.), in which the Greek women compel the men to put an end to the Peloponnesian War by going on a sex strike.

9. Drew A. Hyland, "Plato's Three Waves and the Question of Utopia," *Interpretation* 18, no. 1 (1990): 91-109; hereafter cited in text.

10. The three waves are mentioned at 5.313, 366, and 393 in the *Odyssey*; a fourth wave slams Odysseus against the rocks of Scheria at 5.424-25.

11. On the similarities between the *Republic* and the *Assemblywomen*, see Adam, 1:345-55.

12. Cf. Euripides, *Hippolytus*, 618-24 (where Hippolytus dreams of getting children by buying them from the gods in exchange for gold, iron, and bronze), and *Medea*, 573-75.

9. Philosophical Imagination and Prophecy

1. I have capitalized "Form" in those contexts in which the term appears to be synonymous with "Idea."

2. Klein, 112-25. The following discussion of the Line relies heavily on Klein's analysis.

3. Seeing double is associated with Mystery initiation in Euripides' *Bacchae* (918-20), where Pentheus perceives double images as he comes under the power of Dionysus and begins to move beyond the limitations of his old, conventional vision.

4. In this instance I have followed the text of *Platonis Opera*, vol. 4, ed. John Burnet (Oxford: Oxford University Press, 1902); Bloom concurs with Adam in reading that "they would hold that they are naming these things going by before them [*ta parionta*] that they see."

5. See pp. 32-39 of Jacob Howland, "The Cave Image and the Problem of Place: The Sophist, the Poet, and the Philosopher," *Dionysius* 10 (1986): 21-55.

6. The Socratic philosopher is an intellectual midwife (*Theaetetus*, 149aff).

7. Socrates' inclination at the beginning of book 10 to keep silent concerning Homer out of friendship and respect for him recalls his earlier hesitation, "for Homer's sake," to criticize Homer's representation of Achilles for not being holy (391a).

8. Illuminating accounts of the role of the Good and the Ideas in philosophy and the philosophic life may be found in David Lachterman, "What Is

'The Good' of Plato's *Republic?*" in *Four Essays on Plato's "Republic,"* 139-71, and Mitchell Miller, "Platonic Provocations: Reflections on the Soul and the Good in the *Republic,*" in *Platonic Investigations,* ed. Dominic J. O'Meara (Washington, D.C.: Catholic University of America Press, 1985), 163-93.

9. A complete defense of this seminal point emerges in the course of the debate between Leo Strauss and Alexandre Kojéve in Leo Strauss, *On Tyranny,* 1963; revised and expanded edition, ed. Victor Gourevitch and Michael S. Roth (New York: The Free Press, 1991), 133-212. The Strauss-Kojève debate constitutes a profound discussion of many of the issues at stake in the *Republic,* including the difference between philosophy and sophistry and the relationship between philosophy and politics.

10. Philosophy and Necessity in the Myth of Er

1. Scylla, Socrates' central example, claimed the lives of six of Odysseus's men (*Odyssey,* 12.245-59). In its use of Homeric imagery to represent the dangers of erotic appetites, this passage should be compared with Socrates' reference to the Lotus Eaters at 560c.

2. Further problems are raised by Socrates' use of a human being to represent a part of the human soul. Is the human being within the soul itself composed of parts, including a human being, a lion, and a monster?

3. See *Everyman and Medieval Miracle Plays,* ed. A. C. Cawley (New York: Dutton, 1959).

4. Adam notes that "the two parts of the description [of the cosmos in terms of the column of light and the spindle of Necessity] cannot from their very nature be combined into a coherent and consistent whole" (2:441). This incoherence may be intentional, as is in my view Er's vagueness about the contribution of Necessity to the motion of the cosmos.

Selected Bibliography

Primary Works

Plato

Greek Texts

Politeia. In *Platonis Opera*. Vol. 4. Edited by John Burnet. Oxford: Oxford University Press, 1902.

The Republic of Plato. 2 vols. Edited by James Adam. 2d ed. Cambridge: Cambridge University Press, 1963.

Translations

Plato. 12 vols. Loeb Classical Library. Cambridge, Mass.: Harvard University Press, 1914-27.

The Republic of Plato. Translated by Allan Bloom. New York: Basic Books, 1968.

Other Greeks

Ancilla to the Pre-Socratic Philosophers. Translated by Kathleen Freeman. Cambridge, Mass.: Harvard University Press, 1977.

Aristophanes. *Clouds*. In *Four Texts on Socrates: Plato's "Euthyphro," "Apology," and "Crito" and Aristophanes' "Clouds."* Translated by Thomas G. West and Grace Starry West. Ithaca, N.Y.: Cornell University Press, 1984.

_____. *Aristophanes*. 3 vols. Translated by Benjamin Bickley Rogers. Loeb Classical Library. Cambridge, Mass.: Harvard University Press, 1924.

Aristotle. *Aristotle: The Politics*. Translated by Carnes Lord. Chicago: University of Chicago Press, 1984.

———. *Nicomachean Ethics*. Translated by Martin Ostwald. Indianapolis: Bobbs-Merrill, 1962.

———. *Poetics*. Translated by W. H. Fyfe. Loeb Classical Library. Cambridge, Mass.: Harvard University Press, 1932.

Diogenes Laertius. *Lives of Eminent Philosophers*. 2 vols. Edited and translated by R. D. Hicks. Loeb Classical Library. Cambridge, Mass.: Harvard University Press, 1938.

Herodotus. *The Persian Wars*. Translated by George Rawlinson. New York: The Modern Library, 1942.

Hesiod. *Theogony* and *Works and Days*. In *Hesiod, the Homeric Hymns, and Homerica*. Translated by Hugh G. Evelyn-White. Loeb Classical Library. Cambridge, Mass.: Harvard University Press, 1914.

Homer. *Iliad*. Translated by A. T. Murray. 2 vols. Loeb Classical Library. Cambridge, Mass.: Harvard University Press, 1924.

———. *Odyssey*. 2 vols. Translated by A. T. Murray. Loeb Classical Library. Cambridge, Mass.: Harvard University Press, 1919.

Lysias. *Oration 12: Against Eratosthenes*. In *Lysias*, edited by W. R. M. Lamb. Loeb Classical Library. Cambridge, Mass.: Harvard University Press, 1930.

Plutarch. *The Rise and Fall of Athens*. Translated by Ian Scott-Kilvert. Harmondsworth: Penguin, 1960.

The Complete Greek Tragedies. 4 vols. Edited by David Grene and Richmond Lattimore. Chicago: University of Chicago Press, 1959.

Thucydides. *Thucydides Translated into English*. Translated by Benjamin Jowett. Oxford: Clarendon Press, 1881.

Xenophon. *Memorabilia*. In *Xenophon*, vol. 4, *Memorabilia, Oeconomicus, Symposium, Apology*. Translated by E. C. Marchant and O. J. Todd. Loeb Classical Library. Cambridge, Mass.: Harvard University Press, 1923.

Secondary Works

Books

Averroes. *Averroes on Plato's "Republic."* Translated by Ralph Lerner. Ithaca, N.Y.: Cornell University Press, Agora Paperback Edition, 1974. A medieval Islamic philosopher's "Platonic" commentary on the *Republic*. Noteworthy for its defense of the theoretical life and its reflections on the political significance of the relationship between philosophy and religion.

Bloom, Allan. *The Closing of the American Mind*. New York: Simon & Schuster, 1987. A defense of the Socratic search for wisdom that explores the impediments to education in contemporary life.

Burkert, Walter. *Homo Necans: The Anthropology of Ancient Greek Sacrificial Ritual and Myth*. Translated by Peter Bing. Berkeley: University of California Press, 1983. A study of fundamental aspects of Greek religion that includes a useful account of the Eleusinian Mysteries.

Comotti, Giovanni. *Music in Greek and Roman Culture*. Translated by Rosaria V. Munson. Baltimore: Johns Hopkins University Press, 1989. A useful and engaging introduction to music in antiquity.

Frame, Douglas. *The Myth of Return in Early Greek Epic*. New Haven, Conn.: Yale University Press, 1978. A philosophically stimulating exploration of the myth of return, with special attention to the *Odyssey*.

Kierkegaard, Søren. *Philosophical Fragments*. In *Philosophical Fragments/Johannes Climacus*. Vol. 7 of *Kierkegaard's Writings*, edited and translated by Howard V. Hong and Edna H. Hong. Princeton: Princeton University Press, 1985. Contains a profound interpretation of the nature and implications of Socratic pedagogy.

Klein, Jacob. *A Commentary on Plato's Meno*. Chapel Hill: University of North Carolina Press, 1965. An outstanding example of the kind of careful reading called for by the Platonic dialogues. Includes illuminating reflections on the interpretation of Plato, the meaning of philosophic recollection, and the image of the Line.

Medieval Political Philosophy. Edited by Ralph Lerner and Muhsin Mahdi. 1963. Ithaca, N.Y.: Cornell University Press, Agora Paperback Editions, 1972. The selections from Alfarabi and Maimonides reflect the influence of Plato on medieval Islamic and Jewish political philosophy.

Nichols, Mary P. *Socrates and the Political Community: An Ancient Debate*. Albany: State University of New York Press, 1987. Includes a thoughtful interpretation of the *Republic* as a response to Aristophanes' *Clouds*.

Nietzsche, Friedrich. *The Birth of Tragedy*. In *The Birth of Tragedy and The Case of Wagner*. Translated by Walter Kaufmann. New York: Random House, Vintage Books, 1967. A profound interpretation of Greek tragedy as the most adequate manifestation of the fundamental structure of experience, which is determined by the interplay of "Dionysian" and "Apollonian" principles. Nietzsche anticipates Nussbaum in arguing that Socratic philosophizing is deficient precisely to the extent that it is antitragic.

———. *Twilight of the Idols*. In *The Portable Nietzsche*. Translated by Walter Kaufmann. New York: Penguin Books, 1976. Develops Nietzsche's notion of the "Dionysian philosopher." Includes a section on

The Republic

"The Problem of Socrates" that should be compared with the discussion of Socrates in *The Birth of Tragedy*.

Nussbaum, Martha C. *The Fragility of Goodness: Luck and Ethics in Greek Tragedy and Philosophy.* Cambridge: Cambridge University Press, 1986. An ambitious and insightful study of Greek tragedy and philosophy. Nussbaum breaks with traditional Anglo-American Plato scholarship by reading the dialogues against the backdrop of tragedy.

Planinc, Zdravko. *Plato's Political Philosophy: Prudence in the "Republic" and the "Laws."* Columbia: University of Missouri Press, 1991. Attempts to read the *Republic* and the *Laws* as an extended, philosophic analog of the *Odyssey*.

Platonic Writings, Platonic Readings. Edited by Charles L. Griswold, Jr. New York: Routledge, 1988. A fine collection of essays on the interpretation of Plato, with emphasis on the problem of the dialogue form. Contains debates between representatives of rival modes of interpretation, as well as an extensive, annotated bibliography.

Popper, Karl. *The Open Society and Its Enemies.* 2 vols. 1943. Princeton: Princeton University Press, 1966. Written during World War II, this book links Plato with fascism. Students of Plato are obliged to come to grips with Popper's influential criticism.

Rahe, Paul A. *Republics Ancient and Modern: Classical Republicanism and the American Revolution.* Chapel Hill: University of North Carolina Press, 1992. The first part of this book provides the best discussion available in English of the distinctively political lives of the classical Athenians and Spartans. An invaluable resource for anyone studying things Greek.

Rosen, Stanley. *Hermeneutics as Politics.* Oxford: Oxford University Press, 1987. Chapter 2 ("Platonic Reconstruction") is a succinct Platonic response to Derrida's reading of Plato; chapter 3 ("Hermeneutics as Politics") illuminates the profound significance of the Strauss-Kojève debate.

Strauss, Leo. *The City and Man.* 1964. Chicago: University of Chicago Press, 1978. Includes a classic essay on the *Republic* as well as interpretations of Thucydides and Aristotle's *Politics*. Strauss's careful reading takes seriously the dialogue form and Plato's use of irony.

_____. *On Tyranny.* 1963. Edited by Victor Gourevitch and Michael S. Roth. New York: The Free Press, 1991. Includes Strauss's translation and detailed analysis of Xenophon's *Hiero*, a "Socratic" dialogue about the relationship between the lives of the philosopher and the tyrant that may fruitfully be studied in connection with the *Republic*, and Alexandre Kojève's provocative essay "Tyranny and Wisdom," which interprets philosophy and tyranny as two closely related manifestations of the quest for recognition. The debate between Strauss and Kojève that is included in this volume is exemplary for its philosophic depth and clarity. It centers on the basic issues at stake in the *Republic*, including the difference between philosophy and sophistry and the relationship between philosophy and politics.

Articles, Chapters in Books, and Reviews

Bloom, Allan. "Aristophanes and Plato: A Response to Hall." In Allan Bloom, *Giants and Dwarfs*, 162-76. New York: Simon & Schuster, 1990. An illuminating overview of Socratic pedagogy in the *Republic*. Bloom argues that we must pay more attention to the comic dimensions of the Platonic dialogues and the serious dimensions of Aristophanes' comedies.

Brann, Eva. "The Music of the *Republic*." *In Four Essays on Plato's "Republic": Saint John's Review* 39, nos. 1 and 2 (1989-90): 1-103. A penetrating study of the *Republic* along the lines of Klein and Strauss that is especially valuable for its elucidation of the structure of the *Republic*.

Clay, Diskin. "Reading the *Republic*." In *Platonic Writings, Platonic Readings*, edited by Charles L. Griswold, Jr., 19-33. New York: Routledge, 1988. Clay reflects on the significance for our interpretation of the *Republic* of the constant challenges and interruptions to which Socrates is exposed.

Derrida, Jacques. "Plato's Pharmacy." In *Disseminations*, translated by Barbara Johnson, 61-171. Chicago: University of Chicago Press, 1981. This fascinating and provocative essay attempts to show that Plato's presentation of philosophy as an antidote to the "poison" of sophistry erases or "deconstructs" itself. Especially noteworthy for its careful exploration of the ambiguity of the Platonic texts.

Dimock, G. E., Jr. "The Name of Odysseus." In the *Odyssey*, edited by Albert Cook, 406-24. Norton Critical Edition. New York: Norton, 1974. A classic essay on the *Odyssey* as a quest to "win one's soul." Dimock's reading provides a suggestive introduction to the philosophical dimensions of Odysseus's voyage.

Griswold, Charles L., Jr. "Plato's Metaphilosophy: Why Plato Wrote Dialogues." In *Platonic Writings, Platonic Readings*, edited by Charles L. Griswold, Jr., 143-67. New York: Routledge, 1988. A careful examination of Plato's style that defends the dialogue form on philosophic grounds. Griswold explains the dialogue form in terms of Socrates' "dialectical" attempt to justify the philosophic life. Includes persuasive criticisms of Jacques Derrida's reading of Plato.

_____. Review of Martha Nussbaum, *The Fragility of Goodness. American Scholar* 57, no. 2 (1988): 314-20. Criticizes Nussbaum for her failure to take the dialogues seriously enough as works of literature.

Howland, Jacob. "The Cave Image and the Problem of Place: The Sophist, the Poet, and the Philosopher." *Dionysius* 10 (1986): 21-55. A detailed interpretation of the Cave image, paying particular attention to its dramatic dimensions.

_____. "Philosophy as Dialogue: Charles L. Griswold, Jr.'s *Self-Knowledge in Plato's 'Phaedrus.'* " *Reason Papers* 17 (1992): 113-34. Compares several contemporary approaches to the interpretation of Plato, including those of Nussbaum and Derrida. Includes some discussion of the relationship between Aristophanes and Plato and of the interpretive implications of traditional assumptions about Platonic chronology.

_____. "Re-reading Plato: The Problem of Platonic Chronology." *Phoenix* 45.3 (1991): 189-214. Useful for its criticism of contemporary Plato scholarship in the light of richer, ancient interpretive approaches to Plato. This article argues in particular that contemporary assumptions about Platonic chronology are without foundation.

_____. "Socrates and Alcibiades: Eros, Piety, and Politics." *Interpretation* 18, no. 1 (1990): 63-90. A study of Plato's *Alcibiades II* that focuses on the nature of Alcibiades and compares his quest for honor with the Socratic, philosophic life. Helpful in understanding the related character of Glaucon, as well as that of Socrates.

Hyland, Drew A. "Plato's Three Waves and the Question of Utopia." *Interpretation* 18, no. 1 (1990): 91-109. Hyland shows that while Socrates wants seriously to claim that the first "wave of paradox" in book 5 is both possible and beneficial, his treatment of the second two waves indicates that neither of them are either beneficial or possible.

_____. "Why Plato Wrote Dialogues." *Philosophy and Rhetoric* 1 (1968): 38-50. A clear and thorough introduction to the complex issue of Plato's philosophic style.

Lachterman, David. "What Is 'The Good' of Plato's *Republic*?" In *Four Essays on Plato's "Republic": Saint John's Review* 39, nos. 1 and 2 (1989-90): 139-71. A provocative discussion of the nature and goodness of the Good.

Miller, Mitchell. "Platonic Provocations: Reflections on the Soul and the Good in the *Republic*." In *Platonic Investigations*, edited by Dominic J. O'Meara, 163-93. Washington, D.C.: Catholic University of America Press, 1985. An illuminating account of the Ideas and the Good as the enabling conditions for inquiry.

Page, Carl. "The Truth about Lies in Plato's *Republic*." *Ancient Philosophy* 11 (1991): 1-33. A careful reading that opens up the meaning of key passages concerned with lying in the City of Adeimantus. Page mounts a Socratic defense of the role of lying in the formation of the virtues.

Roochnik, David L. "The Riddle of the *Cleitophon*." *Ancient Philosophy* 4 (1984): 132-45. A discussion of the character of Cleitophon in the

Republic and the *Cleitophon*. Roochnik elucidates the significance of Cleitophon, a radical relativist, for our understanding of the limitations and presuppositions of philosophic discourse.

———. "The Tragic Philosopher: A Critique of Martha Nussbaum." *Ancient Philosophy* 8 (Fall 1988): 285-95. Roochnik argues that Nussbaum pays insufficient attention to the dialogue form, and that Plato is falsely described by Nussbaum as "the great enemy of Greek tragedy."

Rosen, Stanley. "The Role of Eros in Plato's *Republic*." *Review of Metaphysics* 18 (1965): 452-75. An important exploration of the role of *erōs* in the *Republic* that begins by distinguishing between the "mathematical" and "poetical" inflections of *erōs*. Includes insightful comments on the relationship between the *Symposium* and the *Republic*.

Rosenstock, Bruce. "Rereading the *Republic*." *Arethusa* 16, nos. 1 and 2 (1983): 219-46. Reflections on the philosophical significance of the narrative structure of the *Republic*. Of particular interest with regard to the Festival of Bendis and the Myth of Er.

Saxenhouse, Arlene W. "Comedy in Callipolis: Animal Imagery in the *Republic*." *American Political Science Review* 72, no. 3 (1978): 888-901. Saxenhouse demonstrates the comic character of book 5, paying special attention to parallels between Socrates' discussion of the Kallipolis and several Aristophanic dramas.

Seaford, Richard. "Dionysiac Drama and the Dionysiac Mysteries." *Classical Quarterly* 31, no. 2 (1981): 252-75. An inquiry into the thematic importance of the Mysteries of Dionysus in early tragic drama. This article helps to clarify the nature of tragedy as well as the Mysteries.

Segal, Charles. "Transition and Ritual in Odysseus' Return." In the *Odyssey*, edited by Albert Cook, 465-86. Norton Critical Edition. New York: Norton, 1974. A study of the meaning of symbols and rituals of transition in the *Odyssey* and other epics of return. Helpful for the interpretation of symbols of transition in the *Republic*.

———. "'The Myth Was Saved': Reflections on Homer and the Mythology of Plato's *Republic*." *Hermes* 106, no. 2 (1978): 315-36. By reading Plato against the backdrop of Homer, Segal is able to offer many profound insights into the nature of Plato's "philosophic epic."

———. "The Phaeacians and the Symbolism of Odysseus' Return." *Arion* 1, no. 1 (1962): 17-64. This article lays out the structure of the *Odyssey* as a return to reality from the realm of fantasy. Important for understanding the parallel structure of the *Republic*.

Vernant, Jean-Pierre. "Greek Religion." In *The Encyclopedia of Religion*, edited by Mircea Eliade, vol. 6, 99-118. New York: Macmillan, 1987. A superb general introduction to Greek religion.

_____. "Tensions and Ambiguities in Greek Tragedy." In Jean-Pierre Vernant and Pierre Vidal-Naquet, *Myth and Tragedy in Ancient Greece,* translated by Janet Lloyd. New York: Zone Books, 1988. Vernant brings out the ambiguity and tension at the heart of Greek tragedy in a way that underscores the philosophic nature of tragic drama and helps us to appreciate the tragic character of the *Republic.*

Zeitlin, Froma. "Playing the Other: Theater, Theatricality, and the Feminine in Greek Drama." In *Nothing To Do with Dionysus?*, edited by John J. Winkler and Froma I. Zeitlin. Princeton: Princeton University Press, 1990. A study of important dimensions of Greek tragedy that reinforces many of Vernant's insights. Like Vernant, Zeitlin stresses the essentially philosophical nature of tragedy.

Index

Achilles, 99–100; shade of, 137, 143, 144

Adeimantus: "arrests" Socrates, 110; clings adamantly to justice, 84, 160; criticizes poeticoreligious tradition, 77–78, 84–86; defends Glaucon, 84–86; as dreamer, 100; embodies persuasion, 36, 37; moderation and decency of, 85, 96, 100, 101, 103, 108; raises issue of happiness, 40, 107; reforms religious myths, 97–98. *See also* City of Adeimantus

Adrasteia, 111, 112

Aeschylus, 3, 19, 111; *Prometheus*, 111

afterlife, 34, 60, 61, 62, 85, 143. *See also* Hades

Alcibiades: associates with Socrates, 15; compares Socrates with satyrs, 31; embodies spiritedness, 99; loves honor, 8

Alkinoos: and Arete, 53, 117; as

image of philosopher-king, 117; tale of, 49, 53, 155

animals: in Cave image, 133, 135; differ from humans in soul, 87, 113–15; humans bred like, in City of Adeimantus and Kallipolis, 29, 39, 52, 93, 95, 113–15; lack logos, 69–70; in lottery of lives, 156; members of City of Pigs resemble, 91; rulers treat ruled as, 73; Socrates assimilates humans to, in *Clouds*, 14–15, 29; unmusical nature of, 102. *See also* dogs

aphrosunē. *See* folly

Apollo: Socrates' hymn to, 26; oracle of, at Delphi, 105

appetites: assimilation of *erōs* to, 115; tyrannical, 38–39, 58–63; in City of Pigs, 90; community as means to gratify, 37; *erōs* transcends, 38; formation of, 151; good life as

Index

Index

Gilgamesh, 47, 48

Glaucon: ambition of, 9, 79; attached to *nomos*, 91; attitude toward logos, 80; corrupted by tradition, 84–86; courage of, 77, 80, 82, 126; defends moderation, 110; erotic nature of, 78–83, 103, 120; feverish soul of, 78–83, 90–92, 103, 127; identified with Kallipolis, 41; loves honor, 83; philosophic potential of, 77, 79–80, 82, 88, 93, 126; is a poet, 79; praises money, 83, 85; praises tyrannical injustice, 29, 39, 42, 44, 79, 80–84, 98; resembles Guardians, 95; spiritedness of, 37, 94; taming of, 94–110, 160

gods: bribery of, 60–62, 83; in Noble Lie, 105–106; Olympian, 4–5, 40, 143; poets depict as unjust, 62, 78, 82–86; replaced by Ideas, 40, 96–98, 119. *See also* divinity

Good, 45, 51–52, 88, 109, 119–27, 131, 132, 133, 141, 144, 145–46, 148

Guardians: breeding of, 114–15; female, 111–13; inculcated with opinion, 41, 96, 104; are potentially immoderate, 99–100, 103; are potentially vicious, 96, 97, 102, 105–107. *See also* dogs; education

Gyges' Ring, Myth of, 80–84, 92, 98

gymnastic, 92, 96, 98, 102–103, 113

Hades, 15, 29, 43–49, 51, 54, 58, 60, 81, 137, 143, 151, 157

happiness, 39, 40, 54

harmonic modes, 100, 101–102, 104

harmony: of form and content, 34;

moderation as, 108; of philosophical and spirited natures, 102; is not polyphony, 108

health: of polis, 55; in City of Pigs, 88–89, 91; music and, 98

Heracleitus, 96, 156

Heracles, 47, 54

hermeneutical circle, 124–26, 142, 147–48, 160

Hermes, 87–88, 126

Herodotus, 3, 4

Hesiod, 40, 43, 78, 84, 90, 97, 119, 141; Golden Age of, 89; *Theogony*, 4; *Works and Days*, 105

homecoming, Odyssean subtext of, 48, 49, 51, 52, 53, 88, 110

Homer, 3, 4, 40, 43, 119, 141; and Apollonian impulse, 19; corrupting influence of, 65, 78, 84–85; *Iliad*, 4, 8, 45, 53, 56, 90; *Odyssey*, 4, 32, 47–54, 70, 87–88, 94, 110, 137, 144; Plato adapts epic of, 30–31, 44; as prophetic poet, 141–44; Socrates' friendship for, 143

honor, love of, 6, 8–9, 66, 69, 72, 74, 75, 76, 79, 83, 86, 90, 136, 137, 140, 152, 159

hubris, 100, 111

humanity: *erōs* a mark of, 87, 89; philosophy incorporates, 142, 145

Hyland, Drew A., 115, 117

Ideas, 40, 41, 51, 87, 98, 117, 119–49, 151. *See also* divinity; gods

idiōtēs, 7

imagination. *See eikasia*; images

images: Apollonian, 19; philosophical, 119–22, 125–32, 146–49; of prophetic poet, 141–44

imitation: gods not worthy of, 40;

Index

Whitehead, Alfred North, 13
Whole, 49, 50, 124, 127, 129, 131, 133, 134, 144–49
women, 16, 29, 41, 110–16

wonder, philosophic, 36, 37, 55, 82, 96

Zeus, 4, 9, 14, 57, 97

The Author

Jacob Howland is assistant professor of philosophy at the University of Tulsa, where he is a member of the Classics and Honors Programs. He has taught courses on Plato, Aristotle, Greek tragedy, ancient Greek, and nineteenth-century philosophy, in addition to special seminars on topics ranging from nihilism to Socrates. He holds a Ph.D. in philosophy from the Pennsylvania State University and a B.A. in philosophy from Swarthmore College. His publications in philosophical, classical, and literary journals include articles on Plato, Hegel, and Richard Wright, and he is currently at work on a book manuscript, *Philosophy and Politics in the Philosophic Trial of Socrates*.